6 Rules Every Man Must Break

6 RULES EVERY MAN MUST BREAK

[BILL PERKINS]

TYNDALE HOUSE PUBLISHERS, INC.
Carol Stream, Illinois

Visit Tyndale's exciting Web site at www.tyndale.com

TYNDALE and Tyndale's quill logo are registered trademarks of Tyndale House Publishers, Inc.

6 Rules Every Man Must Break

Designed by Ron Kaufmann

Some of the names in this book have been changed to protect people's privacy.

Library of Congress Cataloging-in-Publication Data

Perkins, Bill, date.
   6 rules every man must break / Bill Perkins.
      p. cm.
   Includes bibliographical references.
   ISBN-13: 978-1-4143-1140-1 (hardcover : alk. paper)
   ISBN-10: 1-4143-1140-0 (hardcover: alk. paper)
   1. Christian men—Religious life. I. Title. II. Title: Six rules every man must break.
BV4528.2.P48 2007
248.8'42—dc22   2006033333

Printed in the United States of America

12   11   10   09   08   07
7   6   5   4   3   2   1

To you,
dear child,
who awakens
with
empty hands
empty arms
empty hopes
and
an empty heart.
God hears your cry
gathers your tears
and sends his love.

CONTENTS

ACKNOWLEDGMENTS

BEFORE THE SHOW BEGINS . . .
LET THE CREDITS ROLL

Cindy . . . the gorgeous woman who read every line of this book aloud, often more than once, so I could hear the cadence . . . and for her vigorous challenge of my thinking that keeps me true to God's Word.

John Van Diest . . . thanks for believing in my writing. I hope you're right. John, do you know what they call a short Dutchman? A minivan. That you are not!

Jan Long Harris . . . who kept reminding me as I wrote what could be a controversial book: "Bill, never forget that your job is to help me keep mine." Jan, you're a brilliant editor and funny too. Ummm . . . you've still got your job, don't you?

Kim Miller . . . Wow! Thanks for smoothing out the bumps on the road. This book reads easier because of your work . . . and more work . . . and more work. I'm afraid to ask, but could I make one more change?

Kevin Troudt . . . Mr. Inventor . . . you're a creative genius. It's gonna be be-yig . . . real be-yig! I mean what God's gonna do through you. (Read this with a strong southern drawl). Thanks for letting me share your story with the world.

Ben Smith . . . Hey, doc. Did we have fun as kids, or what? Thanks for our story and letting me tell it.

Mike Temple . . . If anybody knows Mike (see page 19), give him this book. Mike, do you remember that night?

Rod Cooper . . . thanks for opening the door for me. I'll never forget.

Dave Carr and Tim Maxwell . . . for reading portions of the book and giving me some tips to improve them. Dave, can you believe we've been friends so long? Tim, you should be on the radio. What a voice! I tried to copy your deep bass voice, but everyone said it sounded like I was trying to copy someone else's deep bass voice.

Paul Perkins . . . okay, you were right. And I'm glad I listened to you.

Ryan, Serene, Elija, and Sitara Perkins . . . even though you didn't help with this book, I want to thank each of you because I know you would have if you could have. So . . . thanks! You've certainly filled my life with joy.

David Perkins . . . you were right about the last chapter which is now the first chapter being the first chapter instead of the last one. Thanks. And thanks for reading so many of the chapters to me.

Past and present members of the board of White Horse Ministries (Million Mighty Men): Bob Bobosky, Rod Cooper, Jerry Hay, Bob Jesenik, Richard Probasco, Paul Saunders, Phil Shaffer, Brad Nydahl. Thanks for urging me to get out of the boat and trust God for a bodacious dream.

Brett Rademacher and Rick Salz . . . thanks for being God's provision when I first stepped out of the boat and faithful friends since.

Dr. David Blakeslee . . . thanks for being my friend until I needed a therapist and as my therapist helping me roll over. You'll be glad to know my soul stopped tingling.

Gary Witherall . . . I wish I had taken the leap with you. How about if we jump off that bridge together?

Mr. Neeners . . . You dog, you.

INTRODUCTION

A DOG NAMED EL NIÑO

After my friend Rod Cooper read an early draft of the first few chapters of this book I asked, "What do you think?"

"I think you've got an issue with rules," he said.

Of course, he was right. I've always had an issue with rules . . . especially rules that serve no legitimate purpose. I've got an even bigger problem with people who make it their job to enforce those rules.

One day I stood in line at a government building waiting for a lady behind a window to stamp a piece of paper. I don't remember any of the specifics like the time of year or what purpose the paper served. I clearly recall waiting with ten or so other men and women for the moment when I would be first in line and get my paper stamped.

Suddenly, the lady with the power to stamp or not to stamp stomped out of her office and into the hall. She wore her gray hair in a bun pulled tight behind her large meaty head. She stood with her hands on her sizable hips. Sweat beaded her forehead, and her gray dress fit as smartly as the uniform worn by a soldier in a parade.

Pointing at us with the metal stamping device that she held in her right hand, she said, "You must form a straight line if you want me to stamp your paper."

In that moment I squinted to see the stripes on the shoulders of her dress. I didn't see them but felt an urge to stand at attention and snap a quick salute. I restrained myself because I sensed she might not see the humor in my act. And she might not stamp my paper. Instead I got in line directly behind the man in front of me. I must confess something that still bothers me many years later—perhaps "amuses me" would better describe my feelings. When she wasn't looking, I quickly stepped out of the line and incited others to join in my rebellion. We managed to get back into a perfect line before she glanced our way. We giggled conspiratorially each time she looked up and saw us standing at attention in a line as straight as a heavily starched pair of pants.

ADD-ON RULES

That event occurred so long ago it's no more of a memory than a faded picture. More recently I rested in a comfortable chair at the Admirals Club at Chicago's O'Hare International Airport. (Because I travel so much, it makes sense for me to pay an annual fee so I have a place to rest, shower, and check my e-mail during flight layovers.) As you'll discover in this book, I'm notorious for losing things, so I didn't panic when I failed to see my carry-on bag at my side. Instead, I retraced the steps I had taken since I entered the Admirals Club. When the bag still eluded my eye, I approached the agent at the front desk and asked if anyone had turned in a carry-on bag with my name on it. She said nobody had, and then she searched for it. I mean this woman spent fifteen minutes looking for my bag like a drug-sniffing dog at a crack house.

Hoping someone had turned it in at the admitting desk, I took the elevator down and asked that agent if she had seen it.

She said, "Someone from the food concourse called and said they had your bag."

Filled with optimism I walked to the food concourse and found the teenage girl who had cleared my table. When I asked about my bag she pointed to the manager, a short and talkative man, who had locked my carry-on in a closet. As he handed me the bag, he said, "I took it to the admitting desk and suggested the agent page you, but she refused."

Curious about this, I returned to the club and asked the agent why she hadn't kept my bag and paged me. She said, "Because there are one hundred other men with your name in the club."

While I hadn't counted, I suspected no more than one hundred men, women, and children were in the club as we spoke. And unless there was a national meeting for people with the same name, I'm sure there were not one hundred men named Bill Perkins in the club. But since I've always found the agents and service team at the Admirals Club to be gracious and helpful, I decided not to jerk her chain too hard. But I did have two questions for her: "How many of the hundred men named Bill Perkins do you think are missing their carry-on?"

Before she could respond, I asked, "Is this an Admirals Club rule or is this just a rule you've created yourself?"

When I returned home, I called the head of customer service for the Admirals Club and asked her that same question. Would you like to guess the answer? The Admirals Club has no such rule. It was an add-on rule formulated and enforced by one agent.

I've got to admit that in the larger scheme of things, it was no big deal. I could have lost my bag and never retrieved it. So what? Or I could have flown to a distant destination without my clothes and toiletries. Such a loss would have been nothing more than a short-term expense and inconvenience.

But some of the extrabiblical rules—read "add-on rules"—written and enforced by religious leaders and groups can cost you much more. They can cost you the vitality of a growing and dynamic friendship with God. Why? Because they flow from a religious culture that insists you must keep add-on rules in order to grow spiritually. Such rules will pull you down and away from God like lead shoes on a swimmer. And that's why I wrote this book. I think it's time men recognize the difference between legitimate, God-given rules and illegitimate, man-made ones.

We must draw a distinction between the moral law of God that Jesus reinforced and the add-on rules that he resisted. Rules which the apostle Peter condemned when the sect of the Pharisees demanded that Gentile believers be circumcised and obey the law of Moses. Peter asked the same question we must ask: "Why are you now trying to out-god God, loading these new believers down with rules that crushed our ancestors and crushed us, too?" (Acts 15:10, *The Message*). Today, as then, God's grace has liberated us from trying to win his favor by keeping a set of rules.

I believe we must follow the example of Jesus and Peter and fight for the grace of God. We must dialogue with and resist those who create and enforce religious add-on rules. And we must be willing to break them.

THE JOY OF FREEDOM

Okay, you may wonder where I dreamed up the six rules every man must break. Actually, I used a very pseudoscientific process. I submitted thirteen rules to a group of men from a variety of backgrounds and asked them to identify the six most important ones. From their responses, as well as my own instincts, I selected the six rules found in the book.

In case you think I'm going to give you six rules to replace those you should break . . . I'm not. This book isn't about a new set of rules but about the cultivation of a friendship with Jesus Christ. He alone changes us, not a set of rules.

And yes, I can honestly say I have achieved the lofty standard set by this book about as well as I walk on water and refrain from profanity when I smash my thumb with a hammer. Choosing a friendship with God rather than a life of rules and regulations is a lifelong process. But I promise you this: If you read this book and seek to apply what you learn, you'll discover a freedom that will surprise you with joy. (For further insight and motivation, check out some books I've found helpful on page 129.)

Yesterday I took my son's dog, a Chihuahua named El Niño (whom we call Mr. Neeners), for a walk along the shore of the Willamette River. Yeah, I know . . . what "man" would admit that his son owns a Chihuahua and that he takes it for a walk? Quite a contrast for a guy whose last dog was a 185-pound Great Dane named Big. I used to think a Chihuahua, which at six pounds weighs twice as much as the average human brain, was nothing more than an animal with the nervous system of a Great Dane compressed into a dog the size of a large rat. But now that Mr. Neeners and I are friends, I actually like the dog. He's smart, and unlike other Chihuahuas I've heard about, he doesn't snap at people with bared teeth or bark incessantly.

Anyway, as we walked along the rocky shore he tugged on the leash . . . pulling to get free. Finally, I unclipped the leash from his collar. Liberated, Mr. Neeners jumped around, gave high fives to the other dogs, leaped high into the air, and performed a backward flip followed by a perfect four-paw landing. He then sniffed the water, barked at the ducks, and chased a ball.

As I reflect on the undiluted joy of my liberated little friend, I can't help but think about the joy you'll experience when you unclip the leash that holds you in check. If you crave the joy that comes with freedom, turn the page and read about the first rule you must break.

For Discussion

1. What healthy rules did you grow up with? What unnecessary rules do you remember from your childhood?

2. Can you name a senseless rule that you've come up against in the last month or two? Explain.

3. Why are God's moral laws so important?

4. How do his laws differ from man-made add-on rules?

5. What do you hope to get out of this book?

1

THE RULE OF PASSIVITY

NEVER GET IN A FIGHT

Then he said to the man, "Stretch out your hand." So he stretched it out
and it was completely restored, just as sound as the other. But the Pharisees
went out and plotted how they might kill Jesus.

MATTHEW 12:13-14

The junior high I attended in Roswell, New Mexico, allowed students to leave campus for lunch. Normally that worked well, but not always. One day my friend Ben Smith and I exited Al's, a local hamburger joint, after downing a burger and some fries. Here's where the "not always" part happened. As we stepped outside, six or seven older guys with bad intentions met us. Specifically, they had bad intentions for me.

Jerry Ralston, a kid older and meaner than the rest of us, a kid who had repeated several grades, a kid I did not want to fight, shoved me in the chest. Before I could react, one of his assistant assassins grabbed my shirt by the back of the collar and ripped it open. Ben, sensing nobody had any interest in him and realizing he could get hurt, took off . . . a course of action I never let him forget.

One benefit of the surprise attack was that I didn't have time to fear anything. If I had known Jerry planned on ambushing me after lunch, I would have been freaking out all morning. Of course, at the time of the fight I hadn't yet identified that benefit. To this day I don't know why, of all the kids in the school, Jerry selected me for such special attention.

Anyway, I would have run like Ben but Jerry's cohorts had formed a circle around me and I couldn't get away. That disappointed me, because while I might not have been tougher than Jerry and his friends, I knew I could outrun them. I thought about falling down and playing dead, like a possum, but figured they'd never buy that act. So I did the only thing I could do. I fought.

I actually surprised myself, as well as Jerry and his friends, by landing a couple of punches. But every time I hit Jerry, someone would grab at my shirt—eventually ripping it off. Or one of his buddies would shove me from behind. Somehow I lost the shoe off my right foot and one of his wannabe-tough friends threw it on the roof of the hamburger joint. Realizing Jerry couldn't lose and wanting to get back to school, his friends declared him the winner.

I'm sure I looked cool walking back to school with my shredded shirt and single shoe. When we were across the street from the campus, Jerry grabbed my arm. The two of us stopped while his gang ran across the street and headed into the school. That's when he said some unkind words about me and my mother, told me he really didn't like me, and threatened to seriously injure me at a later date.

A QUICK ASSESSMENT

It's funny how quickly I assessed the situation—pros and cons and all of that—and arrived at a decision. If I could have thought that quickly in the classroom I would have made straight As. On the "hit him now" side of the ledger I put: avoid days, weeks, months, years, or decades of paralyzing fear; hurt him enough that he won't want to fight me again; let him beat me now and get it out of his system; my shirt is already shredded, my shoe is on the roof of Al's hamburger joint, and I've already got a bruised face. On the "walk away" side of the ledger I put: hmmm—I couldn't think of a single reason not to finish the fight since he was alone without his support team.

He was as surprised by my right fist to his left cheek as I was by his earlier ambush outside Al's. Before he could recover I had pummeled him with punches. At about that time a teacher saw the fight, raced across the street, and broke it up.

Of course, nobody but the teacher had seen the last round, so the buzz at school was that I had been beaten to a pulp by Jerry. I didn't care. He knew. I knew. And I hoped he'd never bother me again because I feared the guy. That's right. Remember, he was older and bigger than me and had a bad reputation.

A few weeks later Ben and I were at the YMCA playing hoops when Jerry entered the gym. Ben was nice enough to say, "Hey, Jerry, Perkins said you weren't as tough as everybody thinks and that he ripped you apart."

I looked at Ben, dumbfounded. Had he really said that? Sure, I had told Ben—my confidant, my partner in crime, the guy I hung with all the time—that I had taken care of Jerry. I trusted Ben because, well, because I knew his secrets and he knew mine. Yes, I had bragged to Ben that I had beaten Jerry. But every day when I saw Jerry at school, I felt a rush of fear. And now terror fueled by adrenaline raced through my body. My heart rate must have jumped to at least two hundred beats per minute.

While I stood both dumbfounded and terrified, Jerry did the unexpected. He seemed uncomfortable . . . uncertain what to say. So he said nothing. He smiled a cocky smile and walked away. Jerry never bothered me again.

LIFE'S A BATTLEGROUND

From my fight with Jerry, I learned that life is a battleground. And not all fights can be avoided. But it seems as though followers of Christ are expected to be so humble, so meek, so mature, so passive, so submissive, that men sometimes try to avoid a fight at all costs. (I realize that this lengthy list may seem extreme to you, but a lot of guys believe that's what Christian men are like, and they want no part of it.) After all, won't a truly humble and believing man trust God to fight for him? I read somewhere that churches are filled with nice people learning from other nice people how to be nicer people. And nice people don't fight. I'm not talking about whether Christians should go looking for a fistfight. I'm talking about whether Christians should defend themselves or take on an evil or misguided opponent. I'm talking about whether believers should break the law of passivity and get in a fight.

My concern about the passivity of Christian men goes back a long time. I had only been a believer a year or so when I saw Joel Walters, a Christian friend from Austin, Texas, where I was living at the time, attacked by a guy in the parking lot of his apartment building. Joel was an athletic guy with a strong build. As he opened the door to his Volkswagen, a fellow about his size, wearing jeans and a T-shirt, approached him. The two exchanged heated words and then the stranger popped Joel in the nose with a quick right. Instead of defending himself, Joel stood with his hands at his side and said, "I'm a Christian. I don't fight."

From across the parking lot I thought I must have misheard him. But Joel said it again, "I'm a Christian. I don't fight." The guy hit him again and walked off.

I remember thinking that Joel didn't fight because he was afraid to fight. I figured he used his faith to cover his cowardice. But later he expressed pride about the fact that he let some guy hit on him without fighting back. Joel talked as though his passivity proved his devotion to God. But I never believed him. And I still don't. He was afraid to fight because he figured he would get hurt less if he took a punch or two without defending himself. I believe that attitude produces passive men who are easily pushed around and taken advantage of. And that mind-set carries over to other areas of life.

Yes, I know people like to point to Matthew 5:39, where Jesus urged his followers to turn the other cheek when hit on the face. As I pointed out in *Six Battles Every Man Must Win*, I don't believe Jesus was telling us not to defend ourselves.[1] I think he was teaching us not to allow someone to control our behavior. If I'm hit and retaliate, the person who hit me has control over my behavior. Jesus wanted his followers to submit to him, not to their passions or the threats of an enemy. Retaliation puts us under the control of the attacker, not Christ. He also wanted to break the cycle of violence—revenge that still racks the Middle East today. The only way to break this is a heroic "turning of the other cheek."

About now you may be wondering if I'm suggesting we start a Christian version of *Fight Club*. In that movie Brad Pitt plays the part of soap salesman Tyler Durden, who created a fighting club for men as a way of escaping the boredom of their lives.

No, that's not what I'm saying at all. What I am driving at is this: As followers of Christ we need to realize that we're warriors in a battle between two opposing kingdoms. We're in a battle between light and darkness . . . good and evil . . . between God and his army of angels and Satan and his legion of demons. For God's kingdom to advance, his followers must enter the fray and fight. Could you imagine an army in which the troops are taught *not* to fight? We need to break the law of passivity and fight.

For God's kingdom to advance, his followers must enter the fray and fight.

It might surprise you that the two battles I think followers of Christ most need to fight are legalism and hypocrisy. Yet they are the very ones Jesus engaged in.

FIGHT LEGALISM

Take an hour or so and read through the Gospels. As you do, note how many times Jesus hammers away at drunks, prostitutes, crooked politicians, dishonest businessmen, drug addicts, con artists, gays, and thieves. Your list will be short . . . very short. That's because Jesus didn't fight with these people, he hung out with them. The people he challenged were the legalistic religious leaders.

Many churches today have that turned around. They condemn sinners, and their members hang out with the civilized—should I say legalistic—elements of the church. Many of these religious folk attempt to live up to the add-on rules of their church . . . often unsuccessfully. And many live in fear that someone will catch them breaking those rules.

Resist the Spiritual Police

After picking up a few items at the grocery store, I got in the checkout line behind the pastor of a large church. Although we're friends, I could tell he didn't want to talk. He seemed to be avoiding me like a man who sees his former boss, the one who fired him for padding his expense account.

As he stood in line putting his items on the conveyer belt, he awkwardly slipped a bottle of Cabernet onto the belt—as though he were buying Just For Men, Rogaine, or Preparation H and didn't want me to notice.

"Looks like a great dinner," I said.

"I'm on vacation. The wine is for dinner at my home . . . just my wife and me."

I looked down to see if I was wearing a uniform and badge. He seemed to have identified me as a member of the spiritual police and acted as if I had caught him breaking the rules and would soon ticket him.

I tried to think of something cool to say, but couldn't. So I just said, "Oh."

As I climbed in my car, I could identify with that pastor's fear. I remembered an experience I had over fifteen years ago in an upscale restaurant in Lake Oswego, Oregon, the city where I lived and was pastoring a church at the time. As I looked around at the people enjoying lunch, I asked myself, *How many of these people would I feel comfortable inviting to my church?* I concluded I wouldn't ask any of them. Why? Because I didn't think the church culture would provide a safe point of entry for them. Many of these people were drinking beer or wine with their meal. At the time if I drank a glass of wine, I would have to do so in the privacy of my home. I feared the spiritual police might disapprove of my freedom. I understood how that pastor felt . . . and I was glad I had finally decided not to let legalistic people control my life.

Recognize Add-On Rules

But Jesus did more than that. He fought the Pharisees, those who had burdened the Jews with legalistic rules that they had added on to God's commands. He assertively took the battle to them. The opening sentences to this chapter tell the story of the man whose hand Jesus healed on the Sabbath (Matthew 12:13). The Lord knew his act would violate their add-on rule and so he broke it intentionally. How did they respond? They conspired to kill him.

On another occasion the religious leaders protested when the Lord's disciples violated the tradition of the elders by not washing their hands before eating bread. This add-on rule was more than a parent's reminder for their kids to wash up before a meal. Jewish tradition demanded that the faithful wash before and after every meal and whenever they came home from town. And they had to wash according to very strict ceremonial restrictions. Don't underestimate how important such traditions were to most Jews. They would rather walk miles to water than incur guilt by not washing their hands.

Later, when the religious leaders asked Jesus why his disciples violated this tradition of the elders (read: add-on rules), he didn't rebuke his disciples and tell them to go clean up before dinner. Instead, he asked the religious leaders why they violated the command of God for the sake of their traditions. Jesus reminded them that God commanded them to honor their parents. Yet the Pharisees taught people to tell their needy parents that all they possessed had been dedicated to God. According to their tradition, anything pledged in that way—whether it was given or not was irrelevant—could not be given to the parents. In that way, the tradition freed a man from his responsibility to obey God's command and care for his parents.

Jesus then turned to the crowd and explained that true defilement comes from within a man—from his heart, not his hands. A man can't be defiled by eating with unwashed hands, but by an evil heart filled with evil thoughts. This contradicted the Pharisees, who thought only that which touched them from the outside could make them unclean. Since they meticulously followed their traditions and kept themselves clean on the outside, the Pharisees believed they pleased God.

It seems odd to me that the disciples somehow thought Jesus was unaware of how his words affected the religious leaders. They remind me of a kid in the back of a class who raises his hand to state the obvious: "Do you know that the Pharisees were offended when they heard this?"

Not backing off, Jesus said, "Leave them; they are blind guides. If a blind man leads a blind man, both will fall into a pit."[2]

ACT BOLDLY

Why did Jesus fight so tirelessly against legalism? Because he knew it substitutes rules for a friendship with God. It exchanges external conformity for internal obedience. It creates fear and steals joy. The problem persists today. Because men will always add on to grace, the battle will never end.

Legalism substitutes rules for a friendship with God. It exchanges external conformity for internal obedience.

About five hundred years ago, another man dared to challenge the religious leaders of his day, only to find out how difficult that can be. Martin Luther will always be remembered for posting his 95 Theses to the church door in Wittenberg, Germany, on October 31, 1517. This act served as a challenge to church leaders to debate ninety-five important issues.

Why had he taken that bold step? As a monk in the Roman Catholic Church, Luther had begun teaching on the New Testament book of Romans at the university. As he contemplated Romans 1:17, "The righteous will live by faith," he realized a man was made right with God by faith alone—a truth the church of his day had buried beneath a mountain of greed, corruption, and legalistic false teaching. Most offensive to Luther was the practice of selling indulgences—certificates sold by the church promising to shorten a person's stay in purgatory. Johann Tetzel, whom the pope had assigned to sell indulgences in Luther's vicinity, advertised the certificates this way: "As soon as the coin in the coffer rings, the soul from purgatory springs."

At first the pope said little about the 95 Theses, hoping to suppress Luther's views with silence, figuring if he ignored them, Luther would go away. When that failed, he issued a decree condemning Luther's views and calling on him to recant forty-one of his theological positions. Rather than walking away, Luther publicly burned the papal decree, and he was excommunicated in January 1521. Later that year, when Luther was called to appear before a government body, he again refused to recant. He ended his remarks this way: "My conscience is captive to the Word of God. . . . Here I stand, I can do no other."

A single man passionate about the liberating power of the gospel changed world history because he fought legalism.

Luther loved the power of the gospel more than the civilized and established religion of his day.

Likewise, Jesus fought legalism and loved sinners. He lived and fought and died so men could enter into a friendship with God—on the basis of faith . . . not by keeping a bunch of man-made rules. In the next chapter, we'll explore some of the add-on rules that are worth fighting. But there is another fight that's equally important.

FIGHT HYPOCRISY

I became a full-fledged card-carrying hypocrite while just a child. It happened at an age I can't even remember. But I know I was young—like in grade school. It had to do with swearing, or as we called it back then, cussing.

I don't know who taught me to cuss. I never attended a class or read a book on the subject. But by the time I was in the fifth grade (I'm just picking that grade because it seems as good a guess as any other grade—it could have been sooner), I had a fully developed vocabulary of cusswords. In fact, after that age I never added a single cussword to my vocabulary. What set me apart from my friends was that I cussed all the time *around them*. I doubt that a single sentence left my mouth without a profanity. If those words had been deleted from my conversations, I would have seemed like a rather quiet child.

Know Yourself

While my parents occasionally cussed, they did not approve of such language, so I never cussed around them. And it was easy. I think that's when I realized I had a secret person living inside my outer person. It gave me a sense of power too. I never felt a sliver of guilt about my double life. Occasionally, when I thought my dad had heard me cussing, I felt fear, but not guilt.

While I don't remember learning to cuss, I do remember learning to steal. A couple of older boys encouraged me to go into a grocery store and stuff a few Snickers into my pockets and leave without paying for them.

"What if I get caught?" I asked.

"You won't."

I think I had a natural talent for stealing because it came so easily to me. Just like with cussing, I never felt a tinge of guilt. And then one day I got caught. I was in a grocery store and had crammed so much candy into my pockets they bulged like baseballs.

The manager of the store approached me and asked, "What's in your pockets?"

I cussed to myself, then said, "Candy."

"Where did you get it?"

"Over there," I said as I pointed at the candy rack.

"Put it back," he said. "And don't ever try stealing from me again."

I returned *most* of the candy to the shelf. I figured he'd never think a little kid would actually steal after being caught. But I did.

Now here's the bad part. The manager knew my dad, so I lived in daily fear that he would tell on me. That's when prayer became an important part of my life. I begged God not to let my dad find out. I promised never to cuss or steal again if God would answer this one prayer.

And then the unexpected happened . . . the manager of the

store was killed in a car wreck outside of Roswell. I felt such relief. Dad would never discover my secret. I wondered if God had organized the wreck in answer to my prayers. I didn't think so. Then I felt guilty for feeling so happy that the manager had died. My inner voice told me that anyone who celebrates the death of a man with a wife and kids is a bad person. And yet I knew that I could hide my inner person from my parents and just about anyone else. My parents didn't know the cussing, stealing little kid. Only my friends, like Ben, knew that part of me. And I could even hide my inner person from him.

Recognize the Danger of Hypocrisy

What I discovered as a child all of us realize at one time or another. We're all two people—an inner and an outer person. And we're all capable of pretending to be someone we're not. That's what makes religion dangerous. It trains people to be spiritual hypocrites. It accomplishes this through legalism that provides the external rules and expectations to measure spirituality. Because nobody can see our secret self, if we practice keeping the rules, our outer man will appear good and moral and godly. At home our wives and our children may see the darker person. But they usually won't tell on us. Some of the more shameful behavior—like peeking at porn on the Internet—we hide even from them.

Jesus liked sinners more than the religious leaders because they didn't try to disguise themselves. With them, what you saw was what you got.

A hypocrite is someone who lives a double life. He's a man who is different on the inside than he appears on the outside. I think Jesus liked sinners more than the religious leaders because they didn't try to disguise themselves. They might steal, fornicate, and swear, but they weren't hypocrites. With them, what you saw was what you got.

Because I learned hypocrisy from such an early age, I have to guard myself from it at all times. It's hard because I know how other Christians expect me to think and act. I realize they look to leaders as less sinful than everyone else. Yet I know I'm just as flawed as the next guy. And I know whenever a man pretends to be less marred or more together than others, he lacks integrity. The next time you find yourself thinking a leader is somehow wired differently than the rest of us, remember that the wisest, strongest, and godliest men in the Old Testament . . . Solomon, Samson, and David . . . all fell.

Understand Hypocrisy

Jesus waged an ongoing war against hypocrisy. Toward the end of his ministry, even as Jesus urged the people to obey the law of Moses, he warned them about the Pharisees. And his message was clear:

"Woe to you, scribes and Pharisees, hypocrites."

MATTHEW 23:13

"Woe to you, scribes and Pharisees, hypocrites."

MATTHEW 23:14

"Woe to you, scribes and Pharisees, hypocrites."

MATTHEW 23:15

"Woe to you, scribes and Pharisees, hypocrites!"

MATTHEW 23:23

"Woe to you, scribes and Pharisees, hypocrites!"
MATTHEW 23:25

"Woe to you, scribes and Pharisees, hypocrites!"
MATTHEW 23:27

"Woe to you, scribes and Pharisees, hypocrites!"
MATTHEW 23:29, ALL NASB

I think there are two kinds of hypocrites: the self-deceived and the deceivers. The self-deceived believe the lie about themselves. They have developed such a sophisticated system of self-protection that they are blind to their own flaws. They're like the psychotic actor who believes he is the character he plays.

You may wonder how someone could live like that. I called my friend Dr. Rodney L. Cooper, a clinical psychologist and educator, and asked him that very question. He said they isolate or split off the destructive section of their personality and live as though the behavior driven by that part doesn't define the real them.

"Sounds crazy to me," I said.

"It is," he said. "But we all do it every day."

That statement got my attention. "We do?"

"Sure. We're all going to die but we seldom think about that. We certainly don't live as though we could die at any moment. Self-deceived hypocrites do that with their secret and sinful behavior. They just don't think about it."

That leaves us with the hypocrite who's in touch with his dark behavior and knowingly deceives people into thinking he's better than he is.

"That guy has a seared conscience," Rod said. "He's like the priest who molests children but pretends to care for his parishioners. Or the man who is hooked on porn or addicted to alcohol but serves as an elder in his church."

Since Rod's one of my best friends, I figured I'd ask him a more threatening question. "But I'm a hypocrite sometimes, aren't I? I mean, I know how to be sincere, even if I have to fake it."

"Funny, Perkins," he said. "We're all hypocrites at times. But there's a difference between a man who occasionally acts hypocritically and one who always lives behind a mask."

After hanging up the phone I pondered what Rod had said. I don't know if the Pharisees were self-deceived or deceivers or both. But I know I don't want to be either. I don't want to live with the constant fear that someone will discover the darker, hidden me. Nor could I live with the knowledge that the person my family and friends knows isn't the real me. And in order to effectively fight hypocrisy I've got to continually take a ruthless inventory of my thoughts, words, and deeds. I must live authentically. If I can lie to myself and minimize or justify wrong behavior, then lying to others will be easy.

So how do we fight legalism and hypocrisy? I can tell you what I do.

> ▶ I evaluate my own behavior, asking myself if I'm acting in obedience to a biblical command or a man-made rule. If it's a man-made rule, I want to know if I'm following it out of sensitivity to others or because I fear rejection. The former is a good reason; the latter is ultimately self-destructive.
>
> ▶ I try to assess if I'm pretending to be someone I'm

not. If so, I remind myself that God values authenticity, not hypocrisy . . . and so do I.

But I also need to gently address these issues in others—especially my family and friends.

- ▶ When I see legalism elsewhere, I ask questions and graciously take on the rule. It's one thing to keep my mouth shut when eating—that's good manners—it's another to keep it shut when I see something amiss.
- ▶ I remind myself that Christ called me to a friendship, not a religious system of rule-keeping.

In many respects I think fighting legalism and hypocrisy is like fighting racism. Why? Because everybody denies they're a racist. Have you ever heard someone say, "I'm a racist"? I haven't. Yet, I've heard people talk like racists. And when I've said, "I think you sound like a racist," they've never said, "Of course I do. I am a racist." Nor have they thanked me for pointing out a blind spot. Instead, they've gotten defensive and argumentative.

Christ calls you to a friendship, not a religious system of rule-keeping.

And I've seldom had a clearly legalistic or hypocritical Christian agree with me that he was being legalistic or hypocritical. Instead, he's accused me of straddling the moral fence or judging him. He's argued that his rules are biblical and essential to spiritual growth and purity.

I'd like to know how legalism and hypocrisy got such a stranglehold on Christian men. I'm not sure, but I suspect that religious and well-intentioned men and women put rules into place aimed at protecting weak believers. Such rules made sense, so everyone went along with them. Over time the rules became as authoritative as doctrine.

But for that to happen men who knew the difference between grace and legalism and authenticity and hypocrisy stood back and said nothing. I say it's time for men to follow the example of Jesus and fight this battle. I believe the future health of the church rests on the willingness of a few men to do what's right, not what's easy. And I believe legalism and hypocrisy will gang up to beat you down unless you take the fight to them.

YOU'LL NEVER FIGHT ALONE

I won the fight against Jerry Ralston by standing up to him. A few years later though, I found that sometimes that isn't enough. When I was in the ninth grade, Ron Kompton, a fellow student, despised me. At well over six feet tall and over 200 pounds, Ron looked like a man among boys. His fist seemed as big as my head.

One night at a party, I spotted Ron arriving late. I tried to turn invisible, but under pressure that trick never seemed to work. Anyway, Ron hunted me down and started calling me names and hitting me in the chest with the bridge of his upturned hands. Unlike my earlier fight with Jerry Ralston, I would never so much as lay a finger on Ron. Everyone at the party knew that. And it excited them. They smelled blood—or death—depending on whether Ron was willing to go to prison for murder.

I understood how a bull must feel just before the matador begins his bloody business. As we stood in the front yard of the house with a crowd of kids urging us to "get it on," something totally unexpected happened. Something so wonderful and so amazing and so astounding and so excellent that I knew there had to be a God.

A car screeched to a halt just in front of the house. A moment later the car door opened and then slammed shut, and someone yelled, "Kompton!"

It wasn't Superman or Batman or Spider-Man—it was my friend, at that moment my best friend, Mike Temple. Mike was the only guy in town bigger and meaner than Ron Kompton. Before graduating from high school, Mike made the all-state football team twice as a fullback. Later he played college ball for Oklahoma State. He and I were like brothers, and he enjoyed a good fight. I loved that guy!

Mike pushed his way through the crowd, walked up to Ron, shoved him back hard, and said, "Kompton, if you're going to touch Perkins, you'll have to go through me!"

With a surge of courage and, yes, even cockiness, I said, "That's right, Kompton, and don't you ever forget it!"

Ron started whimpering about how he didn't realize Mike and I were buddies, and he promised never to hassle me again.

I like that story because it illustrates how Jesus fights for me. If I abide in him and focus on our friendship, Christ will assure my victory. Sometimes it takes more than sheer grit and will-power to win a fight—including the one against entrenched legalism and hypocrisy. The good news is you'll never have to fight alone.

For Discussion

1. Matthew 12:9-13 describes what conflict between Jesus and the religious leaders? Why do you think Jesus didn't just walk away when challenged by the Pharisees?

2. Which better describes your spiritual life currently: a friendship with Christ or a religious system of rule-keeping? Explain.

3. Legalism is a form of religion that teaches men are made right with God by keeping add-on rules. Why must you fight such a view? What could happen if you don't? What could happen if you do?

4. How can a legalistic form of religion create hypocrites?

5. As you read this chapter, did you recognize any seeds of legalism or hypocrisy within yourself? What might you do to prevent them from growing?

BREAK THE RULE:

How will you break the rule of passivity and fight legalism
and hypocrisy? Discuss both your attitudes and actions.

2

THE RULE OF PLAYING IT SAFE

NEVER RISK IT ALL

One Sabbath Jesus was going through the grainfields, and as his disciples
walked along, they began to pick some heads of grain. The Pharisees
said to him, "Look, why are they doing what is unlawful on the
Sabbath?" He answered, "Have you never read what David did when
he and his companions were hungry and in need? In the days of
Abiathar the high priest, he entered the house of God and ate the
consecrated bread, which is lawful only for priests to eat. And he also
gave some to his companions." Then he said to them, "The Sabbath
was made for man, not man for the Sabbath."

MARK 2:23-27

If you're a man I need to issue you a warning: Beware . . . if you
decide to follow Christ, there are people who will attempt to slip
a harness over your head and a bit in your mouth. They will do
everything within their power to bridle the emergence of the
wild danger that lurks within you.

They remind me of the people of Churchill, a barren snow-
covered town in the Canadian province of Manitoba. We're talking about people who live way north of just about anybody else
in the world. In the late summer and early fall when the thawed
ice in the Hudson Bay begins to freeze, almost a thousand polar
bears congregate just outside the city. They're waiting for the

ice to freeze enough for them to scamper across it and hunt for seals. In the meantime the massive bears prowl around the landscape, and the town, looking for appetizers before the main course.

In an attempt to protect the people of Churchill, local game wardens catch the bears in corrugated metal culvert traps—sections of culverts open on one end and rigged with a door made of steel bars that drops down when the bear grabs the bait and triggers the closing mechanism. The bear hunters then sedate the white beasts and put them in a bear "jail" where they remain until the bay freezes over. They are then transported by helicopter in nets dangling from the choppers onto the frozen bay.

Meanwhile, thousands of tourists migrate to Churchill to watch the bears up close. Bears are fun to watch, but nobody wants them ambling through their town, checking out their houses and eating their garbage. And of course, nobody wants to be mauled or eaten by a bear either.

Churches claim they want men to join their ranks, but all too often they view them as bears in men's clothing—wild animals that need to be controlled. After all, tamed bears are safer than wild ones. While they're not going to put them in cages or airlift them to a wilderness area, they often seek to domesticate them.

Of course, men aren't like the polar bears of Churchill. They sniff a trap the moment they enter a church or talk with a spiritual game warden. So instead of running the risk of being caught and controlled, they play it safe and leave town. That's a better bet than being tamed, not by God's Spirit, but by a set of rules that churches often use to tame men and measure their maturity.

THE MAN WHO WOULDN'T BE TAMED

Following Jesus demands we break the rule of playing it safe and risk everything in pursuing him. What's amazing to me, and I hope to you too, is that Jesus lived among the religious leaders of his day as a wild bear who refused to be tamed. He never played it safe and resolutely spurned their attempts to domesticate and control him. There were rules they established that he absolutely had to break. And there are rules today that I believe he wants you to break. Or, to put it more bluntly . . . there are rules you *have* to break if you're going to let God's Spirit, not some modern-day Pharisees, tame you. I caution you, if you read the rest of this book, you'll put it down liberated or mad . . . one or the other.

There are rules you have to break if you're going to let God's Spirit, not modern-day Pharisees, tame you.

If you think Jesus called you to play it safe with your life, you're mistaken. If you think he wants you to kick back and allow the spiritual game wardens of the world to domesticate you . . . again, you're wrong. He does not. In fact, he risked his life when he refused to capitulate to the commands of the Pharisees.

You'd think obeying the Ten Commandments would be enough to keep anyone busy, but not the Pharisees. These ancient spiritual police added thousands of minute rules to the moral and ritual code of the Old Testament—rules they diligently obeyed. Rules they harshly imposed. And rules they strictly enforced.

The Pharisees possessed the power to destroy a person's life. And they used that power to wield straitjacket-like control over the masses. We're talking Taliban-like authority. It's no wonder the people cowered before them like an abused dog.

And it's no surprise these spiritual megalomaniacs expected Jesus to stand at attention and salute when they blessed him with their presence. Instead of avoiding or ignoring the Pharisees like he might a hornet's nest, Jesus jammed a stick into their world and ripped it apart.

It's hard to imagine that something like hungry men picking a few heads of grain would trigger a heated confrontation between Jesus and the Pharisees. But the religious leaders itched for an opportunity to point out the lawlessness of Jesus and his disciples. Like grade-school tattletales, the Pharisees pointed at the disciples and accused them of breaking the Sabbath law that forbade working on the Sabbath.

Rather than responding with a limp-wristed "Oops . . . I'm sorry. I'll make sure it doesn't happen again," Jesus stood toe-to-toe with the Pharisees and noted the error of *their* thinking. He showed an impressive mastery of the Old Testament when he defended the disciples by utilizing the very Scriptures the Pharisees used to condemn them.

Jesus reminded them of the time when King David and his hungry troops ate bread that had been dedicated to God (1 Samuel 21:1-6). This wasn't a loaf of Wonder Bread that could be picked up at Safeway. David ate bread that had been served as an offering to God and that the law specified could *only* be eaten by the priests (Leviticus 24:9). Yet no religious leader had ever questioned David's right to eat the consecrated bread and share it with his troops.

In essence, Jesus told the Pharisees, "You're wrong. You misuse those portions of Scripture you think support your rigid rules and you ignore the rest." The fact is, what Jesus and his disciples were doing was permitted in the law (Deuteronomy 23:25). It was the Pharisees' obsession with what constituted "work" on the Sabbath that led them to think Jesus and his disciples were lawbreakers. But rather than entering into a technical debate on what constituted work on the Sabbath, Jesus pointed to David's actions in order to drive home a more important point: Human need can take precedence over the ritual aspects of divine law.

Before the shocked Pharisees could respond, Jesus followed his opening observation with a stunning truth: "The Sabbath was made for man, not man for the Sabbath."

God never intended the law to victimize and enslave men. He established the Sabbath to provide men with rest and refreshment . . . to make life pleasurable. The Pharisees, not God, had turned it into a massive load of dos and don'ts that they strapped on the backs of men like refrigerators.

When Jesus let his disciples break the "No Work On Sabbath" rule, he went public with his revolution against the Pharisees and their rule-keeping system of approaching God. Was he taking much of a risk? Of course!

Considering the Pharisees' reaction to his disciples picking wheat, it's no surprise that a short time later as Jesus entered the synagogue, a delegation of Pharisees awaited his arrival. These guys hadn't come to worship God but to set a trap. When Jesus asked a man with a withered hand to stand in the middle of the congregation, the Pharisees held their breath.

Jesus looked at the Pharisees and asked: " 'Which is lawful on the Sabbath: to do good or to do evil, to save life or to kill?' But they remained silent" (Mark 3:4).

In that moment Jesus could have respected the feelings of the Pharisees and backed off. After all, the man's paralysis didn't demand immediate treatment. It wasn't like he had a severed artery. But Jesus didn't back off. Instead, he did what many Christian men believe is forbidden . . . he got mad and glared at the Pharisees. He then stepped over the line they had drawn and took their unspoken dare.

Jesus threw self-preservation to the wind and did what was right . . . not what was safe. He intentionally disregarded the Pharisees and violated their code of spiritual conduct. He healed the man's hand. And he did it before a crowd of people in the synagogue.

Jesus threw self-preservation to the wind and did what was right . . . not what was safe.

That public act told the Pharisees they would never control Jesus. They believed such insubordination and disrespect for the law had to be addressed. So while the man celebrated the miracle that had changed his life, the Pharisees plotted how they could kill Jesus. Ironically, while they condemned the act of healing on a Sabbath, they had no problem with their Sabbath day conspiracy to commit murder. I guess it didn't require any "work."

It's important for us to remember that Jesus didn't come to abolish the law of God, but to fulfill it (Matthew 5:17). He didn't break God's law . . . just the "add-ons" to God's law. *And he didn't lead a revolution against legalism so you and I could roll over and allow our lives to be controlled by the man-made moral code.*

THE JACK-O'-LANTERN RULE

While pastoring a church, I once talked about making jack-o'-lanterns with my three sons during a Sunday morning service in October. Afterward, a leader cornered me and said, "You'd better not talk about jack-o'-lanterns during your messages again."

"Why not?" I asked.

"Because they have an occultic origin," he said. "There are people in the church who would be offended . . . including me."

"I'm sorry you're offended," I said. "If carving jack-o'-lanterns is wrong for you, then don't do it. For me, they're nothing but empty pumpkins with faces and a candle inside. I'll keep making them with my kids as long as it's fun for them. And I refuse to pretend something is wrong when I don't believe it is."

Suppose someone off the street, a man who seldom if ever attends church, had overheard our conversation. He might have walked away with the idea that Christians don't have fun on Halloween. If he listened longer he might have learned that some of the parents don't let their kids go trick-or-treating, not because they fear poisoned candy, but because they've got the notion that all Halloween activities are satanic.

I know some people truly cannot celebrate Halloween in good conscience. What concerns me is that some guys have concluded that devotion to God is measured by compliance with such man-made rules. And they've decided if that's what it means to follow Jesus—they'd rather not. Or, almost as bad, they know such rules seem extreme, or even silly, but conform to them to avoid offending anybody.

Maybe the jack-o'-lantern rule doesn't connect with you. You may relate better to other man-made rules that are sometimes used to measure spirituality.

THE RULE OF TITHING

Several years ago as we drove along a freeway in Portland, my friend Kevin and I discussed the subject of giving—and what

God wanted from us. He insisted a devoted follower would give at least 10 percent of his income to the local church. Seeking to drive home his point, he said, "I'm a tither and give offerings as well (gifts above the required 10 percent), and I also give to the building fund."

Sensing he had impressed me and no doubt persuaded me to change my point of view, a grin like that on the Cheshire cat covered his face. "What do you think?" he asked.

I liked Kevin, and still do, and felt I needed to be careful how I answered him. Such generosity is rare, but I suspected in his case it may have created some problems with his personal finances.

"That's impressive," I said. "Are you in debt?"

"Yeah, I owe about $10,000 on my credit cards."

"Do you own a home?"

"No. I'm renting."

"Do you have a savings account?"

"No."

"Are you setting aside money to buy a home?"

"No," he said. And then a troubled look furrowed his brow. "I just remembered that I owe the IRS $20,000 in back taxes."

"Do you have medical insurance for your family?"

"No."

We rode side by side in silence for a minute or so. And then I told Kevin something he never expected to hear from a pastor.

"You're giving too much to your church," I said.

Kevin almost lost control of his pickup. "Huh?" he said with a perplexed look on his face. "What did you say?"

"I said you're giving too much. I would counsel you to back way off on your giving. Continue to give, but pay off your debts and save for a down payment on a home."

"You're kidding?" he said. "I've never heard a pastor talk like that."

Kevin had been hammered so long and hard about giving that he felt as flat as one of those pennies that's been run over by a train. And he thought godly pastors beat their people with the principle of tithing until they gave, even when they had no money.

"I'm serious," I said.

I wasn't sure how Kevin had taken my counsel. Later he told me that in the cab of that truck he committed to follow my advice. Two years later he was debt free and in his first house. And in case you think he used my counsel as an excuse to stop giving altogether, he gives more now than he ever did before—in part because once he got his financial house in order, he had more to give.

But he struggled for years with ongoing feelings of guilt. Why? Because he had been taught that God expects all believers to give a minimum of 10 percent of their income *to their local church*, as well as "offerings" above that. In order to drive home the point, his pastor often pointed to Malachi 3:9-10 and said God was accusing the Israelites of robbing him by not paying their tithes.[3]

Such teaching communicates the idea that tithing is a reliable gauge of spirituality. It's not. (Jesus did teach that giving is a valid expression of a man's love for God—but not tithing). Indeed, it measures maturity no better than a thermometer measures weight. *On the few occasions that Jesus referred to tithing it was in a negative context.* And that's why he condemned the Pharisees for meticulously tithing while neglecting justice and a love for God (Luke 11:42).

The Old Testament tithe was instituted when Hebrew worship was centralized during the time of Moses. Its main purpose was to support the Levitical priesthood. The Levites ministered to the people and were prohibited from owning land, which limited their earning potential. God wanted their support to come from those to whom they ministered, much like the direction of Scripture for the church today (see 1 Corinthians 9:1-16 and Galatians 6:6).

Furthermore, it surprises many people to learn that the New Testament contains not a single word commanding or even suggesting that followers of Christ should tithe. That doesn't mean the New Testament says nothing about giving. It speaks clearly. Believers are told to give cheerfully, not grudgingly or under compulsion (2 Corinthians 9:7). Jesus praised both Zacchaeus and the poor widow at the Temple for giving joyfully and generously.

Many followers of Christ, including my wife, Cindy, and I, use the Old Testament tithe as an example to follow, not a rule to be obeyed. Giving is a spiritual discipline that allows us to express that God is first in our lives. We give, not because God needs to receive anything from us—he doesn't—but because of our need to acknowledge that all we have is his. Some people find it motivating to set a goal in terms of the percentage of their income they plan to give. But others, like my friend, tithe to relieve guilt. For them, giving less than 10 percent creates feelings of spiritual inadequacy and failure.

While the Old Testament law compelled Jews to give, the New Testament tells believers to give voluntarily (2 Corinthians 8:3). If a Christian finds joy in contributing 10 percent as most Old Testament saints did, they are free to do so. If they want to

give 5 percent, 15 percent, or 50 percent, they're free to do so
. . . if they're financially able.

So what do you do with the rule of tithing? Disregard it.
Ignore it. Break it. Give freely, generously, regularly, and sacrificially according to your ability—because you
love God, not to keep a man-made rule.

*Give freely,
generously,
regularly,
and sacrificially
according to
your ability—
because you
love God, not
to keep a man-
made rule.*

THE RULE OF ABSTINENCE

The surprise people have when they come into
my home is the room to the right of the entry. It
has burgundy walls, a fireplace, a view of Mount
Hood, a three-foot-tall cigar store Indian, a gun
rack on the wall with four rifles, three leather
chairs, a large HDTV, and a high-powered ven-
tilation system that would pull the hair system
off a member of the hair club for men.

The room is a man room. I got it in exchange for a house . . .
seriously. Several years ago my wife said we *needed* to move into
a larger home. I didn't want to move. I liked our old house. We
had lived in it eighteen years and I had grown attached to it.

Cindy had felt cramped in our home since my dad had
moved in with the two of us, our two sons, and our Great Dane.
I think the location of my office bugged her the most. It occu-
pied a significant corner of our bedroom. In order to get to her
chest of drawers she had to climb over me—or have me roll my
chair out of the way. Since I liked it when she climbed over me,
I often resisted moving.

Day after day she pleaded with me. Day after day I resisted.
Finally, in a weakened state of mind I said, "Okay. We can move
on one condition."

She smiled—knowing she had won. I smiled—knowing I had won. "I want a cigar room in the new home."

"Not in my home," she said.

I said okay and went back to work.

"It'll stink."

"Not if it's properly ventilated," I said.

Cindy got her home and I got my cigar room. And I'm pleased to tell you that I have smoked cigars in that room and enjoyed a glass of wine with some great Christian guys. In fact, some of them are Christian leaders who keep their cigar smoking and wine drinking in the closet.

If you attend a church that forbids such practices, you'll understand their paranoia—I mean concern—about how *some* people would react if they found that out. Many Christians regard such practices as ungodly. I realize that by taking on this issue I'm trying to move an elephant out of the church's living room with a skateboard. But I think it's a crucial issue to address because it illustrates an unbiblical form of legalism.

Please don't misunderstand me. I've written three books on compulsive and addictive behavior and realize the dangers of drunkenness and other forms of addiction. I used to ask the men whom I interviewed to serve on a church board if they ever drank alcoholic beverages. If they said they did, I asked if they would be willing to abstain during their term of service. I asked the question just to find out how important alcohol was to them. If they said they would abstain, I never asked them to do so. But if someone was unwilling or unable to give up something like alcohol for a period of time, I believed it might have been too important to them. And I asked more questions.

Some Christians argue that because alcohol is so easily

abused, a godly Christian would never drink it. But if you follow that line of logic, you'll also conclude that since sex is so easily abused by so many people, a godly Christian would also abstain from all sexual activity. Or since money can so easily corrupt, a godly Christian will stay poor, or become poor if he's rich. Yet nobody would say that about sex or money. God intended money, sex, and alcohol to be blessings to man. And they are a source of blessing when used within the boundary of his moral law.

Let me give you another example of how such boundaries can be maintained. Like a lot of people, I enjoy coffee. In fact, I roast green coffee beans that come from places like Panama, India, Uganda, and Kenya.[4] I enjoy grinding the beans and smelling their rich aroma. I have fun making espresso, lattes, cappuccinos, Americanos, and French pressed coffee. I think you get the idea that I like coffee. With that in mind it might strike you as odd that I only drink coffee on Sundays and Wednesdays. Why? Because I don't want to get addicted to caffeine. As with tobacco (cigars) or alcohol (wine), I believe moderation is the best course of action.

Would I try to impose my personal coffee practice on someone else? Of course not. That's just the way I manage my coffee intake. Likewise, I'm simply suggesting churches not supervise the eating or drinking habits of their people. Those who believe, based on their reading of Scripture, that they should not drink need to honor that conviction. They should not, however, view their personal position as mandatory for all believers. I'm convinced the Holy Spirit will produce godliness in a believer as he strengthens his friendship with Christ and abides in him. Jesus, not rules, brings about true godliness.[5]

I know many Bible teachers insist the alcohol in the New Testament was unfermented grape juice. If so, can you imagine the disappointment at the wedding of Cana when the guests, expecting wine, got grape juice instead? Come on . . . if you read the text it clearly says Jesus performed a miracle by turning water into the best wine served at the party.

If you insist the wine was nonalcoholic then answer this question: How did the Corinthian believers manage to get drunk on the communion wine if it was unfermented grape juice (1 Corinthians 11:21)? How much grape juice would someone have to consume to get intoxicated? If you find out, let me know.

Okay, let's get back to my cigar room and what happens within its burgundy walls and in front of its fireplace. The apostle Paul makes it clear we're not to be mastered by anything or anyone but Christ (1 Corinthians 6:12-13). With that in mind, an addiction to anything (except caffeine or sugar . . . hmmm) is morally wrong. And we all know about the dangers associated with habitual or addictive tobacco use. But what about an occasional cigar? Is that wrong?

The great seventeenth-century preacher Charles Spurgeon caused quite a stir when he said he smoked cigars to the "glory of God." Imagine that! He went on to say, "No Christian should do anything in which he cannot glorify God; and this may be done, according to Scripture, in eating and drinking and the common actions of life."

Spurgeon responded to his critics with these words: "There

> *"No Christian should do anything in which he cannot glorify God; and this may be done, according to Scripture, in eating and drinking and the common actions of life."*
>
> *CHARLES SPURGEON*

is growing up in society a Pharisaic system which adds to the commands of God the precepts of men; to that system I will not yield for an hour. The preservation of my liberty may bring upon me the upbraidings of many good men, and the sneers of the self-righteous; but I shall endure both with serenity so long as I feel clear in my conscience before God."[6]

I applaud Spurgeon's unwillingness to bow to the rules of his critics. In doing so he drew a sharp distinction between the laws of God and the rules of religious men.

THE RULE OF DAILY SPIRITUAL DISCIPLINES

This rule reflects the belief that spiritual disciplines, like daily prayer and Bible study, will inevitably produce maturity. Most mature believers I know *do* try to make prayer and Bible reading a part of their daily routine. They know that the spiritual disciplines are crucial for their growth. But they also know that it is God, not the disciplines, that produces godliness.

Whenever someone establishes a spiritual yardstick based on a spiritual routine, he needs to be careful. Remember, the Pharisees prided themselves in their prayers and scriptural knowledge. In fact, they made it a practice to regularly fast and pray (Luke 5:33). Yet they didn't recognize God when he came down to earth. All over the world people of many faiths diligently pray and read their holy books every day. Such activities no more make someone close to God than reading a stranger's diary makes you his close friend.

It might seem strange to you that I would raise this issue since I conclude *Six Battles Every Man Must Win* by inviting men to join me and commit to practice four daily spiritual disciplines. Yet, I stressed in my book that the disciplines do not create godliness, they create an environment where God's grace can transform a man. I said: "Those of us engaged in the war for our heart must exercise spiritual discipline. We must prepare ourselves for spiritual combat as though our life depended on it. Because it does! . . . While grace is the means by which God changes us, we must prepare our hearts for his grace to be released."[7]

We spend time with God in prayer and reading his Word so we can know him better and love him more—not so others will view us as spiritual.

We spend time with God in prayer and reading his Word so we can know him better and love him more. Not so others will view us as spiritual . . . and not because someone else demands it from us.

OTHER CHRISTIAN ADD-ON RULES

One of my sons lived in a house with some very rigid Christians—I'm talking about a rigidity that would rival a steel pole. One day he walked into the house carrying a hamburger purchased at Carl's Jr. One of the guys got in his face and said, "Don't you ever bring one of those in the house again."

"What are you talking about?" my son asked.

"That!" he said, pointing at the burger as though it were a dead rat.

"Um. Why not?"

"Because Paris Hilton appeared in one of their TV ads."

"Oh! Now I understand," my son said. *You're a total idiot*, he thought.

I could provide a lengthy list of spiritual rules that would be as varied as the groups that enforce them. I know believers who judge others based on such things as:

- ▶ Musical preference
- ▶ Clothing style
- ▶ Expressions of worship
- ▶ Health (poor health shows a lack of faith)
- ▶ Wealth (if you're rich, God has blessed your faith and obedience)
- ▶ Dancing
- ▶ Hairstyle
- ▶ Political views
- ▶ Body piercing and tattoos

That's a short list that I suspect you could expand. I focused my attention on tithing, abstinence from all alcohol and tobacco, and the spiritual disciplines because they're so common. Of course, the immediate response by many who insist on these three standards is predictable: "If you don't live like that, unbelievers will view Christians as no different than the world."

If you think that way I hate to burst your bubble, but unbelievers don't care. It's irrelevant to them how much you give to your church, whether you enjoy an occasional glass of wine, or whether you read your Bible every day. They care a lot more about how you treat them when they work as a cashier at the grocery store, or how you behave at your child's sporting events, or whether you give to the drive to raise money for a local charity.

Yet whenever you challenge an add-on rule, other Christians may express concern that your behavior will cause a "weaker brother to stumble." Part of showing love to others, in fact, is being sensitive to their weaknesses. So of course, everyone should be careful how they act around someone who's recovering from any kind of an addiction. It would be insensitive, unkind, and morally wrong to tempt someone to do something that might harm him. And just because a believer can disregard those man-made rules doesn't give him the freedom to hurt others. My problem with most Christians who insist these rules be followed for the sake of our weaker brothers is this: They would never participate in "questionable practices" any more than they would hang glide or bungee jump. And they want to make sure nobody else does either.

I think many believers handcuff their freedom to the wrist of such spiritual police and live their lives, not pursuing joy, but avoiding an offense against a modern-day Pharisee. They realize that when they break these rules they risk antagonizing people who may then reject them, ostracize them, slander them, and do everything they can to discredit them.

THE YEAST OF THE PHARISEES

So why not just go with the flow? What's the big deal about striving to look spiritual? If you want to be a radical follower of Jesus, that's not an option. He's called you to revolt against such rules. Once after the Pharisees had demanded that Jesus give them a miraculous sign proving his authority, Christ warned his disciples about the "yeast of the Pharisees" (Matthew 16:6). Like someone who doesn't get the punch line of a joke, they stared at each other and wondered if he was warning them against buying bread with defiling yeast in it. After all, they had forgotten to bring bread on their journey across the Sea of Galilee and would have to buy several loaves.

But Jesus wasn't talking about yeast for bread. He used the

word metaphorically in reference to an evil influence that could spread and corrupt anything into which it was inserted, like a drop of arsenic in a glass of milk or a can of Coke. He was talking about the teaching of the Pharisees in which they reduced a man's relationship with God to a set of rituals and rules. Jesus warned about the dangers of buying into that religious philosophy. We need to feel free to break such rules or else they will corrupt our relationship with God.

I'm convinced the legalism among Christians is one of the greatest enemies of the gospel today. It strips believers of joy and reduces their friendship with God to nothing but a set of rules. I hope you don't misunderstand me. This chapter is not about tithing, abstinence, or the spiritual disciplines. It's about identifying man-made rules that add to the law of God and the teaching of Christ. It's about breaking the rule that says, "Play it safe and never risk it all." Christ has called us to a radical faith that fights against legalism and its restrictive rules.

I'm convinced the legalism among Christians is one of the greatest enemies of the gospel today.

RISK IT ALL

Are you ready to take the risks involved in breaking such rules? Like the add-on rules of the Pharisees, they are man-made and have nothing to do with your spiritual growth. In fact, if you're keeping them simply because you think they, rather than your friendship with Christ, will make you more spiritual, you should break them. Why? Because breaking them frees you to follow in the steps of Jesus. Remember, he died for breaking add-on rules, not for keeping them. Shattering these regulations allows you to make a bold statement too: Your friendship with God flows from love, not rules.

On a foggy New Year's Day, my friend Gary Witherall left my home before sunrise, before I had awakened, and drove ninety minutes to a two-hundred-foot bridge in Washington State. Then he jumped off. In fact, he jumped twice. The first time he faced the river below and dove. The second time, he faced the bridge and fell backward into the deep ravine.

Why had an otherwise sane, though a bit crazy, man done such a thing?

"I had to face the fear that tormented me," he said. "I did that by jumping off a bridge and risking my life. And you know what? The moment I jumped—my fear was shattered and I felt alive again."

I gazed with admiration at his Bungee Masters T-shirt. I love Gary, and his words somehow made me happy and sad. You see, his lovely wife, Bonnie, whom I had also loved, had been shot and killed while working in a medical clinic in Lebanon a month before.

"Bill, it was exhilarating," he said in his British brogue. "I was falling and falling and then I felt the bungee cord slow my descent. And then it pulled me up and I got to free-fall again."

He was excited. "The second jump was easier but scarier because I couldn't initially see where I was going."

I was jealous of Gary. In the face of unimaginable pain, he had the guts to do something I've always wanted to do. In fact, it's one of the scariest things I've never done. But I could have gone with Gary. Or I could have jumped with my son David when he made the big leap. Both times I had excuses. Or did I make excuses? I'm not sure. Maybe by the time you read this story I'll have leaped from that bridge. I think if I ever bungee jump, I'll want someone else to go first. It seems like that would reduce the danger. I mean, if the cord proved too long, or not strong enough, or not securely anchored—well, you get the idea.

In a way, that's what makes breaking the rule of playing it safe a bit easier. Others, like Jesus, have already broken it. And I'm convinced that when you take the risk and break the rule, you'll discover what Gary found when he leaped off that bridge—you'll taste life in a new and exciting way.

Of course, you may be thinking—this is a different kind of a life you're talking about, Bill. You're right. And interestingly enough, living it effectively will demand breaking another rule—the rule of perseverance. Turn the page to see what I mean.

For Discussion

1. What does a domesticated man look like? How does he differ from Jesus? How can men learn to put aside the tame life for the Christlike life?

2. In Mark 2 and 3 Jesus stood up to the Pharisees when they accused his disciples of breaking their "no work on Sabbath rule." Why did he resist them? What would a failure to stand up to them have said about what Christ believed?

3. If practicing spiritual disciplines is not the measure of a man's faith, what is?

4. What is the difference between the man who reads God's Word simply to gain knowledge and the one who reads Scripture to strengthen his friendship with God?

5. Name one add-on rule that would be hard for you to break. What risks would be involved in breaking that rule? What benefits? Who might you offend by breaking it?

6. How can we balance the need to keep our weaker brother from stumbling with the need to be free of unnecessary rules? (Consider Romans 14–15; 1 Corinthians 8–10.)

BREAK THE RULE:

What is your strategy to break the rule of playing it safe and take a risk by breaking an add-on rule?

3

THE RULE OF PERSEVERANCE

NEVER GIVE UP

I am the true vine, and my Father is the gardener. He cuts off every branch in me that bears no fruit, while every branch that does bear fruit he prunes so that it will be even more fruitful. You are already clean because of the word I have spoken to you. Remain in me, and I will remain in you. No branch can bear fruit by itself; it must remain in the vine. Neither can you bear fruit unless you remain in me.

JOHN 15:1-4

The ink black BMW Roadster, just off the showroom floor, hugged the road as it screamed around sharp turns on the California mountain road. At thirty-five hundred feet, the driver could see the glimmering ocean to his left. Dense thickets of shrubs and small trees covered the sides of mountains, which were capped with granite and towering pines. On that particular day, he didn't care about the view. He cared about getting around the next turn fast . . . crazy fast. Approaching a turn wide, he drove just a few inches too far to the side of the road. The right front tire slipped off the edge of the asphalt. Proving he could afford a faster car than he could handle, the driver overcorrected, and the high-tech, ultra-expensive car spun around once, flipped three times in the air, landed on its wheels in a cloud of dust, and wrapped itself around a tree.

The driver rocketed out of the car during the first flip, and like an acrobat with Cirque du Soleil, he flew seventy-five feet in the air, landing feetfirst and facedown. He slid across the grassy shoulder of the road, tearing his designer shirt and shredding his $250 jeans, before slipping feetfirst over the side of a precipice. Miraculously, he not only survived but seemed uninjured—except for his neck, which locked in place and prevented him from looking up and down or side to side.

Fortunately, he had grabbed hold of a tiny tree that was growing out of the side of the cliff. He knew that when his weight uprooted the tree, or he became too tired to hold on any longer, he would plummet to a certain death.

Desperate, he cried out to God, "Save me!"

He didn't expect an audible answer. After all, in the past he had begged God to speak to him and never heard a word. To his surprise, a soft baritone voice said, "Let go."

While he knew at the core of his being that the voice was God's, he refused to release his grip on the tiny tree. Indeed, he gripped it more tightly.

Again the voice commanded him to let go. Again he refused.

Twenty minutes later, with sweat covering his body and soaking his clothes, with the muscles of his arms and shoulders cramping, with his hands too exhausted to hold on, he let go.

In the moment between opening his hands and starting to fall, he wondered why God had told him to let go. He wished he had been able to call his wife and kids and tell them he loved them. He wished he hadn't driven so fast. He wished he wasn't so short. He wished his hair transplant looked better. He promised God if he survived he would wear his seat belt next time. He then plummeted wildly—to the wide ledge some two feet below.

I suspect as you finished reading the last chapter you might have been wondering how you can grow spiritually if you decide to ignore or break those add-on rules. After all, you may be convinced that the rules and those who enforce them are seeking to help you harness the wild danger, the emerging evil, the sin within you. You know they're just trying to help you overpower your evil appetites, urges, and habits. Or perhaps they want to prevent such evil forces from getting a foothold in your life. You're convinced their motives are for your good, and I suspect you're right.

You may wonder what would happen if you risked it all and broke the rules. Couldn't you suffer, not only the wrath of the spiritual police, but the consequences of letting your evil appetites run wild? You've repeatedly been told to persevere in your fight against the darkness within. You've been taught to never give up . . . to hold on . . . to hang in there . . . to claw your way to the other side.

I'm here to say that won't work. God is telling you the same thing he told the driver of that black BMW: Let go. Give up the fight. God never told you to win the fight against sin any more than he told you to pin King Kong. On the contrary, he wants you to break the law of perseverance and walk away from that fight. And as you've no doubt guessed, the rest of this chapter will help you do just that.

NEVER SAY THE *D* WORD

My dad possessed the sensitivity of a rhino tiptoeing through a hen house. Coupled with a distorted, or even sick, sense of humor, he unwittingly inflicted emotional pain on his children. As a salesman who traveled extensively throughout much of

Texas and New Mexico, he was frequently gone. Before most trips he'd call me aside, put his strong hands on my head, and say, "I'm going on a long trip and I may get killed in a car wreck. It could be a head-on collision. Or, at night, if a cow wanders onto the road, I could hit it, killing both of us. I might fall asleep and wrap the car around a telephone pole, or drive off a bridge. If I don't die, I'll see you in a few days." He would then climb into his Lincoln and drive away.

His departing words certainly gave me something to think about as I slid into bed at night. Looking back I realize he never intended to prepare me for his death but to create an affection fueled by a fear of losing him. Of course kids, like dogs, will love even the most misguided parent. And I loved my dad. That's no doubt why as a boy I dreaded his impending death—which finally occurred when he was eighty-seven as I stood at his side.

Let's face it: Death isn't the hottest topic at a party. Broach the subject and people will avoid you like a drunken beggar. Just the thought of a close friend or family member dying stirs up anxiety. With that in mind it's easy to understand the fear that wrapped its serpentine tentacles around the disciple's brains and squeezed hard the night before Jesus' crucifixion. Even though Jesus had repeatedly alluded to his death, the truth never got traction in their minds . . . at least not until their final meal together.

I understand the disciples' confusion. What loyal follower of a presidential candidate would envision his death the night before his election? The disciples knew the Pharisees disliked Jesus, but they also knew the people adored him. Hadn't they just wildly cheered him when he rode on a donkey into Jerusalem?

Certainly his popularity would shield him from the wrath of the religious leaders. And they knew a heart attack wouldn't kill him. After all, he was only thirty-three years old and in perfect health. They likely concluded that a man who walks on water, heals the sick, and raises the dead would live long and prosper.

They expected that, before long, Jesus would overthrow the Romans and usher in the kingdom of God. And, of course, he would give each of them a position of power. Such hopes can cause a man's mental radar to detect only those incoming messages that confirm his dreams and to ignore all others.

Maybe the disciples figured Jesus' previous talk about dying referred to some distant event that would occur after he ascended to the throne. But on his final night, there was no getting around his words. He left no wiggle room for another explanation. He said one of them would betray him. Peter would deny him. And he would go away.

THE POWER OF THE VINE
Confused and afraid, the disciples left the upper room and stepped onto the narrow Jerusalem street. The frigid air—just like their growing fear—surrounded them, nipping at their faces and cutting through their robes. Holding their fluttering torches high, they followed Jesus out of the city.

Suddenly he stopped. A key moment had arrived. In the simplest terms, he would tell them a spiritual truth that would produce as much amazement as the first use of numbers or the invention of the wheel—nothing would ever be the same again.

In essence he said, "From now on, I want you to stop fighting to please God by trying to improve yourself and defeat your evil urges. Instead, rely on the fact that as long as we're connected (and we will always be connected), I'll work in you and through you to accomplish my purposes. So instead of fighting to become someone you'll never be and striving to accomplish what you can't achieve, give it up. Relax and rely on me."

Of course, if Jesus had said it like that, the disciples might have missed the point. And so he took a grapevine in his hand and said, "I am the vine, you are the branches; he who abides in Me, and I in him, he bears much fruit; for apart from Me you can do nothing" (John 15:5, NASB).

I like the disciples, because like me, they weren't the sharpest students in the class. On numerous occasions Jesus told them something, only to find that they saw his meaning as well as a blind man sees a sunset. (Remember their confusion over the Pharisees and yeast?) But the analogy of the vine and branch contains such profound and life-changing spiritual power that Jesus took no chance with the disciples. Just to make sure they didn't miss his meaning or underestimate its importance Jesus used the word *abide* ten times in six verses (John 15:4-7, 9-10, NASB).

Think about it. Jesus could have said, "If you want to be fruitful, clean up your act, perform a religious ritual, tithe, abstain from alcohol, go to church, think positive thoughts, carry a big Bible, put a bumper sticker on your car, and definitely, definitely, stop having fun." Instead he repeated a single word ten times:

Abide

Abide

Abide

Abide

Abide

Abide

Abide

Abide

Abide

Abide

It occurred to me that unlike the Ten Commandments that Moses received on the mountain, Jesus repeated one word ten times. The Israelites were given a rock-hard set of rules. Jesus offered a flesh-and-blood friendship. He knew what the disciples would soon discover and what we must learn. Namely, friendship with him, not iron-willed determination to live up to the standards of God or man, produces a life that pleases God and changes the world.

Christ had a mission for his disciples and he has one for you. Just as soft drink producers use carbonation to jazz up their beverages, Jesus releases us into the world to add life and sparkle—to change it. Yet at the vineyard he stressed friendship, not mission. Why? Because in the spiritual world who you know and how well you know him determines what you will accomplish. All of your skills stand or fall on the foundation of your friendship with Christ. That's the point of Jesus' analogy.

Friendship with Christ, not iron-willed determination to live up to the standards of God or man, produces a life that pleases God and changes the world.

GOD'S WORKING RIGHT NOW

In parts of Oregon, vineyards are as common as cotton fields in west Texas or heat in Arizona or salt in the ocean—well, not as common as the last two, but you'll see plenty of them if you drive around. Almost every day I drive past Oswego Hills Winery. It's a few miles from my home and boasts vine-covered rolling hills, a beautiful barn, and a kaleidoscope of flowers.

Several days ago I saw the vinedresser working among the vines. It's his job to care for the grapevines so they'll achieve maximum fruitfulness. Jesus said that is what his Father, the gardener, does when he lifts up a branch and prunes it.[8] He lifts branches off the ground to protect them from decay and to assure they'll get plenty of sunshine. And he prunes away unproductive offshoots or dead branches. In other words, God is currently at work bringing into your life those people and circumstances needed to nurture your spiritual growth and fruitfulness.

Make no mistake about it; Jesus wants you to bear "much fruit." But what does that mean? I think the apostle Paul sums it up in the nine words he uses to describe a fruitful disciple: "But the fruit of the Spirit is love, joy, peace, patience, kindness, goodness, faithfulness, gentleness and self-control" (Galatians 5:22-23). In other words, we are to draw others to Christ by our attitudes and actions.

LIVE IN RELAXED RELIANCE

I think an honest man would admit he could no more consistently exhibit all of those traits than he could ride a bucking bull. Though I've never ridden one, I've been to rodeos and watched them on television. I've got a lot of respect for men who have the guts, or insanity, to climb on the back of a Brahma bull—an animal that can weigh up to two thousand pounds and doesn't stand still once it leaves the chute. If they stood still,

I'd be inclined to sit on one. But they leap and twist and kick and try to kill the rider once he's off their back.

Anyway, I think an honest man would admit he could no more consistently exhibit *all* nine of those traits than he could ride a bucking bull. Even a rodeo champion only stays on a fighting Brahma for eight seconds or so. And no matter how deep our dedication or determined our efforts, we eventually fall. I know myself and a lot of other guys pretty well, and I'm sure none of us could consistently bear spiritual fruit through self-effort.

Still, many of us believe the lie that says it's our job to tame the beast within and teach ourselves to perform unnatural tricks, like a circus bear that wears a skirt and rides a bike. We believe that's what religion is all about—helping us become better, kinder, and gentler men. And it seems to us that apart from a few men who are just born nice, no man ever accomplished that without consistent effort. And so we give it our best effort, fall on our faces, and get up and try again.

That brings us to the profound truth contained in the analogy of the vine and the branches: God doesn't expect you to become more Christlike on your own. Jesus wants you to allow him to produce the fruit of the Spirit in your life. Your responsibility is to abide in him. Just as a vine provides sap to the branch, so Jesus supplies all you need to bear spiritual fruit. The key to such a life rests on your new identity as a branch and your willingness to do what every fruit-bearing branch does without effort: *abide.*

Jesus used the word *abide* to communicate the idea of his followers living in a friendship of relaxed and effortless reliance on him. Like a branch, we don't need to work to maintain our *connection* to the vine. The moment we trusted Christ as our Savior, we entered into an eternal and never-to-be-broken connection with God. Yet, unlike a branch, we must choose to *abide* in the vine. A man can be "in" Christ without "abiding" in him.

I repeat what I said above: To abide in Christ is to live in a friendship of relaxed and effortless reliance on him. As we abide in him, we don't need to strain to bear fruit.

Jesus used the word abide to communicate the idea of his followers living in a friendship of relaxed reliance on him.

I've often thought it would be cool if animals could talk. I've asked my dog to talk, not bark, on numerous occasions. He just stares at me with a dumb look on his face. I did once try to convince a vegetarian food server that plants could communicate—I'll tell you about that later. While plants can't talk, I know for certain if a branch could talk it would say: "I've got the easiest job in the world. In fact it's not a job at all. I just hang around and allow the life of the vine to pass through me and produce grapes."

According to Jesus, living a fruitful Christian life should be just that easy. Yet why do we find "abiding" so hard to practice? I suspect it's because unlike branches we have a brain, and we think spiritual growth demands striving. Yet Jesus didn't tell us to clinch our fists and lock our jaws and set our feet and grunt and groan and try harder to be better men. He told us to abide in him. And the only way that will ever happen is for us to give up the fight to perfect ourselves and rely on Christ to live through us.

Simple? Yes.

Easy? No.

SPIRITUAL WEIGHTLESSNESS

When I say no, I mean it's unnatural. If it came naturally, every follower of Christ would live such an abundant life that people would race to grab a piece of the action as though it were money falling from the sky. But we can learn to abide in Christ, just as we develop other skills . . . like scuba diving, my favorite sport. Over the years I've learned that experienced divers know a simple practice that is a key to safe and enjoyable diving. It's a hard skill to perfect because it violates everything a man believes about swimming.

If you're a diver, you may know what I'm about to say. If you're not, it may surprise you. The best divers know how to relax when they're underwater. They rely on their buoyancy compensation device (BC) to keep them neutrally buoyant—in a state of weightlessness where they go neither up nor down. For this to occur, a diver must swim underwater—but not like he does on the surface.

Scuba divers are recognizable by the air tank they wear on their backs. The tank is attached to a vest that houses an internal air cell made of tough durable urethane plastic and contains the air that provides flotation at the surface and buoyancy control underwater. A hose runs from the tank to the air cell, and divers use a valve on the hose to control the amount of air in the BC.

Here's how it works. Divers must carry weights on a belt or in pockets of their BC to enable them to descend. When they first enter the water, divers don't want to sink, they want to float, and so they fill the air cell as they wait for the other divers in their group. When they're ready to descend to the world of reefs, sharks, lobsters, and turtles they deflate the BC and head down. Now here's where it gets tricky. If they're still sinking once they're at a depth of say seventy-five feet, they need to add air to their BC until they're naturally buoyant. (People often ask me the deepest I've ever dived—I tell them one mile.)

It's not uncommon for beginners to continually sink because they strap on too much weight and put too little air in their BC. Because they don't know how to properly use their BC and rely on it to do all the work for them, they flail their arms and kick with their feet—not to move forward but to keep from sinking. In the process they kick reefs with their fins, damaging them. They hit other divers with their arms, annoying them. They burn air fast, shortening their dive. And they get tired, increasing their risk of injury. Because they're struggling to keep from going too deep, they feel anxious and uncomfortable and exhausted.

So how does a diver master his buoyancy? In a word: practice. An experienced diver constantly checks his depth gauge to assure he's swimming at a level depth. Anytime he ascends even a few feet, the water pressure decreases and the air in his BC expands. To keep from an uncontrolled ascent in which he rockets to the surface, he must release air from the BC. If on the other hand, he descends, the air in the cells contracts and he'll need to add air or he'll continue to sink.

Master divers swim relaxed in a weightless state with their arms at their side or folded over their chest. Every movement is fluid and easy. They burn air slowly and enjoy the beauty around them. They've learned to rely on the BC to hold them at a steady depth. And I can tell you, diving in a weightless state is like flying over the cliffs and ridges of the deep—it's amazing and exhilarating.

Abiding in Christ is like scuba diving because it requires us to achieve spiritual weightlessness—a state of relaxed reliance on Christ. For that to happen, we must constantly monitor our spiritual gauges. If we're anxious, lustful, bitter, or fearful, then we're not neutrally buoyant. We're not abiding. We don't solve the problem by kicking harder and flailing our arms and trying harder to achieve a better attitude. Spiritual activity, no matter how intense, won't create spiritual weightlessness. Instead, when we sense we're sinking, we must look to Christ and inflate our spirit with his presence. Or, to put it in his words, we must abide—allowing his life to produce the fruit of the Spirit in us.

Spiritual activity, no matter how intense, won't create spiritual weightlessness. Instead, when we sense we're sinking, we must look to Christ and inflate our spirit with his presence.

ABIDE IN CHRIST'S WORDS

So how do I inflate my spirit with Christ's presence? I've got to admit that no matter how many ways the idea is illustrated, it remains abstract and mystical. Jesus did offer some additional insights when he told his disciples, "If you abide in Me, and My words abide in you, ask whatever you wish, and it will be done for you" (John 15:7, NASB). Did you catch that—"if . . . My words abide in you"? Abiding in Christ involves allowing his words to abide in us.

Although Jesus isn't physically with us, his words are. The more we read them, the more they shape our thinking. The more they shape our thinking, the more they should direct our emotions and guide our behavior. In *Six Battles Every Man Must Win*, I noted: "As you experience the goodness of God, you will desire to spend more time with him. You will crave his Word and celebrate the way he uses it to change your life."[9]

Occasionally someone will ask me, "What does it mean for you to abide in Christ?" They may not word the question quite like that. But that's what they mean.

I seldom answer the question quickly. It's not that I don't know the answer. It's that I think my answer may seem a bit odd to most people.

"Umm . . . for me . . . and this might seem different to you . . . but I think about Christ most of the time. That's true whether I'm working out, or driving, or walking, or writing."

I remember a time in my life as a Christian when I wasn't living with an ongoing awareness of Christ. I recall saying to myself one day: *Wow! So this is what it's like not to know God.* It's really weird to me because while I don't remember the exact date of that thought, I know the time of day, season, and location. I was walking across the mall at the University of Texas on an early fall afternoon.

"So that's what it means to abide in Christ?" the person will ask. "You're saying it means to live with an ongoing awareness of his presence?"

And this is the part of my answer that may seem odd. "No. That's not what it means. I can be aware of Christ without abiding in him, just as a man may be aware of his wife and yet flirt with another woman. Abiding in Christ involves an ongoing awareness of his presence, but it also means consciously trusting Jesus to enable me to think and act like him. For me this happens as I saturate my mind with his thoughts. This results from reading and meditating on the Bible and through prayer. God's Word energizes my walk with Christ."

ABIDE IN CHRIST'S LOVE

Abiding in Christ means abiding in his words. But it also means something else. Jesus said, "Abide in My love. If you keep My commandments, you will abide in My love" (John 15:9-10, NASB). Here's where the teaching of Jesus flies in the face of the ancient religious leaders. He taught that the commandments of God reveal the character of a loving God. The more a man abides in the love of God, the more he thinks and lives in a way consistent with the wishes of God. Yet even here he is completely dependent on God's grace: "God is working in you, giving you the desire and the power to do what pleases him" (Philippians 2:13, NLT).

Abiding in Christ involves an ongoing awareness of his presence. It means consciously trusting Jesus to enable you to think and act like him.

From Jesus' perspective, the commandments serve as a loving fence built to protect his children so they can grow strong. And they provide a setting to strengthen relationships. A man who doesn't steal or covet enjoys healthy friendships and families. That means a man who lives within the commands of God is truly abiding in the love of God. And he's discovering how God's love can improve his life.

But for the Pharisees such a concept would settle into their hearts as well as seed on concrete. Because they believed God hated sinners, they saw the commandments as weapons of God aimed at evil people. They used them to exercise control over the masses by fostering guilt and shame. If you think God approves of such a self-serving use of his law, think again. Jesus fired his harshest criticism at the Pharisees and people like them, who "tie up heavy loads and put them on men's shoulders, but they themselves are not willing to lift a finger to move them" (Matthew 23:4).

What angers me most about the religious police is that they have convinced many men that spiritual growth results from trying hard to keep God's rules. Because the emphasis is on using spiritual rules to harness their wild side, many men feel as confident as Tom Thumb trying to ride a Brahma with a steel door on his back.

Jesus came to free men from such heavy burdens. Incredibly, that truth was not always well received. In fact, one day Jesus entered a synagogue in his hometown of Nazareth, picked up a scroll, and read from the prophet Isaiah: "He has sent me to proclaim freedom for the prisoners and recovery of sight for the blind, to release the oppressed" (Luke 4:18). As the crowd watched, Jesus rolled up the scroll, gave it to the attendant and sat down. He then said, "Today this scripture is fulfilled in your hearing" (Luke 4:21).

How did the home crowd respond to Jesus' proclamation? Remember, these folks knew him as Joseph's son who grew up just around the corner. Instead of embracing him and the freedom he offered, they hustled Jesus out of town to a cliff where they intended to hurl him to his death. Instead of zapping them with a lightning bolt, which I might have done, Jesus "walked right through the crowd and went on his way" (Luke 4:30).

That crowd-gone-wild scene demonstrates the radical nature of Jesus' message. When someone understands his words, they're either enraged or liberated. Still, I'm intrigued by the rage of the crowd and their religious leaders. I wonder what made their time bomb tick.

PURE INSECURITY

A number of years ago I suffered from a bout of clinical depression—meaning I was depressed for more than two weeks and it disrupted my life. Because I'm not by nature a depressed guy, I wondered how I got in such a dark place. My therapist, Dr. David Blakeslee, helped me realize I had developed an unhealthy ability to persevere. That's right—I suffered from "I don't know when to quit."

You see, years earlier I had determined that once I started something I would never throw in the towel. After all, I knew if I hung in there long enough I'd outlive most of my problems and competition. Now, twenty years later, I was writing over five hundred words a day for publication (in six years I wrote the equivalent of twenty 200-page books), as well as a sermon every week. I was also leading a church and caring for my family. All of these activities provided me with a growing ministry and a sense of financial security. Oh, and lest I forget . . . burnout.

One day Dr. Blakeslee tilted his head to one side, smiled, and asked: "Bill, if you were sleeping on your arm and it began to tingle, what would you do?"

That was a question I could answer. "I'd roll over."

"That's right," he said. "And yet when you're involved in something that's causing you mental and emotional pain, you refuse to roll over. You refuse to quit. You believe God wants you to hang in there even when it's destroying you."

As he spoke I heard a mental gear fall into place: *cla-clink*. I exhaled so deeply I thought I'd collapse. But he had more to say. And his words were profound: *"Bill, sometimes you need to let go of an impure form of security in order to grab hold of a pure form of insecurity."*

In a flash I saw his meaning—like when you suddenly solve a mind-twisting riddle—only this mattered. I realized that I had held on to work *and* ministry for security. My stubborn unwillingness to let go of one or both had corrupted my soul. I had believed the lie that a growing ministry and financial security would lead to contentment. Stepping away would mean grabbing something less secure that would strengthen my soul. That thought scared me.

Frankly, I didn't know if I had the courage to walk away from my job to pursue something less secure. It seemed almost like bungee jumping without a harness and cord. What if God didn't stop my fall?

I had grown accustomed to sleeping on my arm. Rolling over would mean taking a risk. Yet my soul had gone past the tingling stage; it felt numb and listless. And I had no intention of remaining in the dark and lifeless world of depression. Eventually, I gave up. I quit my writing job and later resigned from the church I pastored to launch a national men's ministry. I took the leap and embraced a new direction that offered no financial security and uncertain success. But I knew I had grabbed a pure form of insecurity.

That experience gives me insight into the Pharisees and the crowd. They put their confidence in an impure system of rules and regulations because they thought doing so would give them security. Then Jesus walked into the synagogue, grabbed the rug on which they stood, and jerked it out from under them by declaring himself to be the Messiah whom they should follow.

The crowd recoiled at the audacity, the impudence, and the brashness of Jesus. They must have wondered how someone so young, inexperienced, uneducated, and local—especially local—could free prisoners, heal the blind, and liberate the oppressed. Accepting his claim would mean abandoning the Pharisees and their rules. The Nazarenes would kill Jesus before letting go of their corrosive beliefs.

How tragic. The people from Jesus' hometown preferred the shackles of slavery to freedom. At the vineyard, Jesus invited his disciples to experience a kind of liberty through his love that would prompt obedience to his commands. His men would keep the commandments, not because they had persevered in their battle against sin or because they had the grit to persist in obeying the commandments of God. Their victory would stem from another reason altogether—they abided in their Lord.

We must decide if we're willing to let go of our own impure form of security in order to embrace Jesus— a pure form of insecurity.

Like the disciples and the men of Nazareth, we're forced to decide if we're willing to let go of our own impure form of security in order to embrace Jesus—a pure form of insecurity. Are we willing to stop relying on our ability to hang in there until we win the battle against sin?

I GIVE UP

By now, you've probably realized that as a boy I got in a lot of fights. Because I avoided fighting with someone bigger, faster, stronger, and tougher than me, I *almost* always won.

After school one day in September, Joe Edwards and I met in the alley behind the Road Kill Grocery Store in Roswell, New Mexico (not its real name, but one that would soon apply to me). Until that fight, not a single loss marred my perfect record.

As a crowd of kids cheered us on, we exchanged blows. Or, to put it more accurately, he pummeled my face while I tried to dodge his jabs and duck his punches. Time and again I saw his knuckles get bigger and bigger a millisecond before they bashed my cheeks, nose, and chin. I could not escape or block his lightning quick jab or crossing right.

After several minutes of combat I concluded he could outbox me, so I took him to the ground. Bad decision. He could also outwrestle me. Somehow I managed to escape his grasp and return to my feet. Feeling like a punching bag, I wished someone would cut me down so I could run away. Nobody did. In fact, my fans, who significantly outnumbered his, urged me to keep fighting. My little sister, Beckie, who viewed me as a better fighter than Zorro, expressed supreme confidence that I would prevail. "Tear his head off!" she of little stature yelled.

Tear his head off, I thought. *Can't you see what's happening? I'm getting killed.*

As much as I hated to admit it to myself, I could not win the fight. No way. And so I did something I had never done before . . . I gave up.

Are you at that place in your life? Can you see that the force of your dark side is too fast and strong for you to overpower? If so, then you're ready to break the rule of perseverance and give up. And in giving up, you'll be ready to do the one thing Jesus wants you to do; the one thing that will give your life meaning and guarantee your fruitfulness; the one thing you can't do until you break the law of perseverance and abide in Christ.

Now that you've learned how to break the first three rules, you'll be ready to break the fourth: the rule of independence.

For Discussion

1. What one thing did Jesus say we must do to bear spiritual fruit? What add-on rules did he not mention?

2. What does it mean to "abide" in Christ? (Note my definition on page 52 and discuss it.)

3. How, specifically, can you practice abiding in Christ?

4. What could happen if you don't abide in Christ?

5. What provides security in your life? How reliable is it for you? What do you fear would happen if you gave it up?

6. What does it mean to let go of an impure form of security and grab hold of a pure form of insecurity? What impure form of security are you holding on to? How can you let go of it and grab hold of Christ?

7. What do you risk by giving Christ the chance to prove himself faithful?

BREAK THE RULE:

How will you specifically break the law of perseverance and give up?

4

THE RULE OF INDEPENDENCE

NEVER ASK FOR HELP

I will ask the Father, and He will give you another Helper, that He may be with you forever; that is the Spirit of truth, whom the world cannot receive, because it does not see Him or know Him, but you know Him because He abides with you, and will be in you. I will not leave you as orphans; I will come to you. After a little while the world will no longer see Me, but you will see Me; because I live, you will live also. In that day you will know that I am in My Father, and you in Me, and I in you.

JOHN 14:16-20, NASB

I once spoke at a large church in Houston, Texas—by large I mean one that drew over ten thousand people every week. Afterward, I met with some of the leadership team.

It didn't take long for someone to ask, "How big's your church, Bill?"

I looked up at the ceiling as I calculated the number. "I'm pretty sure we run somewhere between nineteen and twenty thousand a week," I said.

The entire staff team sat at attention and their eyes opened as wide as saucers. "Twenty thousand a week—why that's . . . that's . . . that's bigger than our church."

I nodded my head and smiled. "Twenty thousand would be.

But I said my church ran between *nineteen* and twenty thousand."

Once they caught the drift of my statement everyone laughed. And I laughed too. But I felt as if a bee had stung me. And I recoiled on the inside because I knew that two decades of ministry had not resulted in what I had once dreamed would take place.

I hate it when I compare myself with a man whose achievements eclipse my own. Such comparisons make me feel small, like a deflated balloon. Yet, as much as I hate feeling inadequate, something good comes from the pain. Namely, I'm reminded that I want my life to make a difference. I want my time here on earth to mean something. If I didn't want my life to matter, then I wouldn't care what I had accomplished.

In that way we are alike. Regardless of your age, intelligence, education, income, or influence, you also want your life to matter. And in some way you question whether or not it does or ever will. You may go for weeks, months, or even years without giving it much thought. And then you run into an old high school or college buddy whose lofty achievements make you wonder how he could have done so much more than you in the same amount of time. You slap him on the back, but inside you're not celebrating his success. You're grieving the comparative smallness of your own—which a few moments before you had viewed with pride.

Too often, well-intentioned Christians have added to my sense of insignificance. While in seminary I led a weekly Young Life club, taught two high school Bible studies, served as the chaplain for the school football team, and taught a Sunday school class at the church I helped launch. Those were exciting days, and I felt good about the work God was doing in the lives of the kids and in the church. One evening I met with the church leaders to see if the church would support my ministry financially.

"We're sorry to say that we can't help you at this time." The words seemed to roll off the board chairman's tongue with such ease. When I spoke I felt as if I had a mouthful of marbles. And my words felt like marbles falling out of my mouth.

"Are you kidding?" I asked. Their decision made no sense to me.

"No, we're serious."

"Why would you *not* support my ministry?" I asked, with emphasis on the word *not.*

"Bill, we question your commitment. You never attend the Sunday evening service."

I sat dumbfounded. I invested almost every waking minute to the ministry, and in the eyes of my church leaders I lacked "commitment" because I skipped church on Sunday nights. It's tough to determine the worth of what you're doing when believers use an add-on list of responsibilities to measure devotion. I meet guys all the time who question the value of their work. And in the spiritual arena, they're not sure how they measure up either.

As men we determine our competence by our ability to master the world around us on our own. In other words, we prize self-sufficiency. With enough time, we like to think we can get the job done—whether it's driving to an unknown location, fixing a broken toilet, closing a business deal, or overcoming a personal weakness. That's why most of us don't appreciate unsolicited advice from others. And it's why most men obey the rule of independence and avoid asking for help.

A MOUSE IN A MAZE

Yet a lasting sense of significance will elude our grasp, like a forgotten dream, unless we find help. But who can help us? Seriously, whom would you look to for an infusion of significance? It's a joke to think the rich and famous could help. We've read about their pain and seen it played out on TV. From the top of the food chain, they look down with despair as they realize all of their accomplishments stand as strong as a New Orleans levee against a category 5 hurricane.

If you're a history buff, maybe you'd look to the ancients for guidance. If so, you'll walk away empty-handed. According to Homer, who wrote in the eighth century BC, Sisyphus was the wisest of all mortals. Yet when he resisted the will of the mythological gods, they sentenced him to ceaselessly rolling a rock to the top of a mountain where it would always roll back down. The gods believed there was no more painful punishment then futile and hopeless labor.

That old story seems as current as today's news. It reminds me of the summer my youngest son, Paul, worked on an assembly line for Nike. Every day, hour after hour, he performed the same task over and over again. He hated the job, not because it was hard work, but because it seemed meaningless.

When the Jewish King Solomon considered all of life, he sounded as if he had just returned from watching Sisyphus repeatedly roll his stone up the mountain or my son inject air into airsoles. He writes, "Meaningless! Meaningless! . . . Utterly meaningless! Everything is meaningless!" (Ecclesiastes 1:2).

Such statements and stories may make you feel like a mouse in a maze with no way out. But there is a way out. Jesus doesn't call us to spend the rest of our lives trying to endlessly jump back and forth over a moral bar. He doesn't call us to tediously obey a list of add-on rules written to hold us in check. And he doesn't call us to work and play and live and die without meaning. He calls us to a life of freedom and joy and purpose. But finding such treasures requires listening to his words and discovering from them how he can add meaning to our lives. It demands breaking the rule of independence and asking for his help.

Jesus doesn't call you to spend the rest of your life trying to endlessly jump back and forth over a moral bar. He calls you to a life of freedom and joy and purpose.

ENDING THE SEARCH FOR SIGNIFICANCE

Before I became a follower of Christ I believed God existed but I didn't think he could be known. And if God couldn't be known then nothing mattered. When I met Christ I discovered God could be known. That realization changed everything . . . if God could be known, then nothing *else* mattered.

I'm sure that after following Jesus for three-and-a-half years, the disciples knew that nothing else in life compared to their friendship with him. His words, his miracles, his laughter, his courage, his love, his prayers, his vision . . . everything about him filled them with life. With him they realized their purpose and destiny. He was the Rosetta stone that unlocked the mysteries of God that gave their life meaning.

But on the night before his crucifixion he told them he would soon leave. And they couldn't follow. It wasn't just that his death would dash their dreams of imminent power and glory. His death would deprive them of the one whose presence infused their lives with meaning and direction. They would be like arrows without a bow.

Jesus knew this, and so he made a promise: "After a little while the world will no longer see Me, but you will see Me; because I live, you will live also. In that day you will know that I am in My Father, and you in Me, and I in you" (John 14:19-20, NASB). Jesus explicitly promised that following his physical departure he would live in each of them through the person of the Holy Spirit—the Helper who would dwell in them forever. Following his death and resurrection, Jesus would actually be closer to his disciples than before.

The search for significance ends not at a place but with a person. The hole in our hearts can't be filled with money or power or fame or family or friends. We can spend the rest of our lives accumulating stuff and building relationships, but we will always be looking for something bigger and better . . . the key we hope will unlock the mystery of life's purpose. And yet as we abide in Christ, we discover that it was the locksmith we needed all the time, not a key.

BUILT TO FLY

My home sits on the side of a steep ravine in Oregon. As I sit at my desk and look out the window to my left, I see two old-growth fir trees and countless other firs, pines, and maples. I slide open my window and hear birds chirping. Several black-capped chickadees dart past and light on a tree. Above the towering firs, wide-winged turkey vultures soar on the thermals.

A person could watch birds his entire life and never realize what a marvel they are. Every part of a bird is designed to enhance flight. Their feathers are lightweight, strong, and aerodynamically shaped. They look solid, but they're not. The spine that runs down the middle of a feather is hollow. And the thousands of barbs that grow on both sides of the spine latch together with hooklets that interlock so tightly that smoke blown at a feather cannot penetrate it. When the wing flaps downward, the feathers come closer together, blocking the passage of air and creating lift. When the wings flap upward, the feathers open up to allow air to pass through.

The feathers on a bird's tail allow it to steer and brake. Their beaks and bones are lightweight. Indeed, the bones of the frigate bird weigh less than its feathers. Because flight requires power, birds have the largest muscle-tissue/body-mass ratio of all creatures. And their circulation system delivers oxygen to those muscles at a wondrous tempo. A sparrow's heart rate is 460 beats a minute, and a hummingbird's tiny heart races at 615 beats a minute.

Yet this special design would be useless without air. It amazes me that something invisible provides the environment in which birds fly. The wings, bones, feathers, lungs, heart, and blood were all designed with air in mind. In essence, the bird finds its purpose in the air. And we find our purpose in the invisible Christ.

No matter how impressive our personal achievements, we will never find lasting significance if we refuse to recognize our dependence on Christ. It's only in him that we can make sense of ourselves—our design—our thoughts and feelings and passions and hopes and dreams. Furthermore, and this is crucial, *as we abide in Christ's presence and trust him to empower our thoughts and actions, he saturates all we think and say and do with eternity.* When we live with a conscious awareness of

Christ's presence, it's as though our lives become a letter that testifies to Christ's sufficiency . . . a letter that will be read for all time.

Once you realize this, you'll know that it's spiritually irrelevant whether you own the bus company, fix broken buses, or drive a route. God places no greater value on running a company than changing a tire. Even the most menial task possesses eternal value if it's done while abiding in Christ. And apart from him the greatest human accomplishments will make no more noise in eternity than a tree that falls in a forest with no ears.

As we abide in Christ's presence and trust him to empower our thoughts and actions, he saturates all we think and say and do with eternity.

Listen, God didn't place eternity in your heart so you could find meaning in perishable things like money and houses and cars and jobs and power. Doing so is like a bird searching for the meaning of its design in a nest. The purpose of a bird is to fly, and the purpose of a man is to abide in Christ. When we fulfill that purpose, we discover the two elements of life that possess eternal value.

ETERNAL ATTITUDES

I've often wondered how attitudes and actions that flow from faith in Christ possess the stuff of eternity. As I've examined the Scriptures and read the thoughts of men much smarter than me, I think I've made some sense of it. Let me try to illustrate it using a story.

Decades ago an artist asked if he could paint a portrait of my wife, Cindy. I agreed with a single condition: I wanted to periodically check up on his progress. He agreed, and every few days I'd drop by his studio. One day I saw something on the canvas that stunned me. He had used gray paint to cover my wife's almost completed mouth. He had ruined the portrait.

"Phil, what have you done?" I asked.

"It wasn't right. The only way I could fix it was to start over."

Sure enough, when I returned a few days later he had captured the joy in Cindy's smile. That large painting now hangs in the library of our home—reminding me of my wife's beauty and the lesson I learned from Phil: The job of an artist is to capture not just the features of a subject, but her heart . . . her essence. I learned that truth, probably for the first time in my life, from Phil Hanks. This experience also helps me understand the work God is doing in us.

When the Bible talks about attitudes and actions that possess eternal value, I believe it speaks of God as a great artist. Every day he dips his brush into the attitudes and actions of our lives that flow from our faith in Christ. He then uses them to create in us the image . . . the essence . . . of his Son. Jesus said "I chose you and appointed you to go and bear fruit—fruit that will last" (John 15:16). In the future, when we possess resurrection bodies, all of creation will see in us the strength, character, and laughter of Jesus.

Indeed, I believe the degree to which we reveal his character will be directly related to how often and consistently we abided in him . . . and allowed his Spirit, the Helper, to work through us. Every time we possess and express the fruit of the Spirit, the Father will add a brush stroke to our eternal images. Our eternal resurrection bodies will differ from each other, and those differences will enable us to glorify God uniquely.

This doesn't mean we lose our identity. God doesn't want to

destroy our uniqueness. Rather, he wants to reveal the character of his Son through us. Could you, through hard work and perseverance, create such beauty and wonder in your life? Of course not! You could no more do that than a portrait could paint itself. And yet God can't create the likeness of Jesus in us until we find our significance in him.

ETERNAL FRIENDS

In addition to changing us, God wants to change the world through us. Specifically, he wants to transform people. He wants to raise the dead and heal the blind and restore the crippled. And while that statement may seem unrealistic or loony, and while God may not actually perform physical miracles through any of us, he does want to use our influence to impart life to those who are spiritually dead, vision to those who are spiritually blind, and healing to men and their families. In the spiritual arena, such transformations demand a miracle as great as turning water into wine or walking on water. Just because we can't see these changes with our eyes makes them no less real or amazing. I've never seen what goes on inside a cocoon, but when a formerly ground-hugging caterpillar emerges as a butterfly, I know a profound transformation has taken place.

Jesus didn't call you to a life of mediocrity and insignificance. He wants your life to matter. He called you to live a supernatural life that changes people for eternity. When Jesus said he called us to bear fruit that will last, he wasn't just talking about our character. He was talking about our friendships too. Remember, only four things last forever: God, God's Word, angels, and people. Of those four we only have a chance to influence one—people.

Because we can't see our friends in their future resurrection garb, we can't grasp how mind-blowing they'll one day appear. We've seen the prince in commoner's clothes for so long we fail to recognize his royalty. Paul put it this way: "The body that is sown is perishable, it is raised imperishable; it is sown in dishonor, it is raised in glory; it is sown in weakness, it is raised in power; it is sown a natural body, it is raised a spiritual body" (1 Corinthians 15:42-44).

Jesus didn't call you to a life of mediocrity and insignificance. He wants your life to matter. He called you to live a supernatural life that changes people for eternity.

Several years ago I visited the giant redwoods and sequoias of northern California with my three sons. As we craned our necks to look up the trunks of those behemoths, all four of us said "Wow!" We marveled at the thought that we were beholding living organisms that predate the birth of Christ. Some of them sunk their roots into the California soil before the birth of Alexander the Great or even Abraham. The oldest known giant sequoia stands almost 300 feet tall and took root during the lifetime of Methuselah some 3,200 years ago. That massive tree has approximately 11,000 cones and will disperse from 300,000 to 400,000 seeds per year. Every dark brown seed is one-fifth of an inch long and one-twentieth of an inch wide with a yellow brown wing on each side.

I suspect if you stood under one of those mammoth trees while tens of thousands of seedy helicopters spun through the air, whipped by the hot, dry wind, you'd marvel at the sight. Even more amazing to me is the fact that each of those seeds houses a giant sequoia. I am staggered by the thought that, just as those massive sequoias sprout from whirling green helicopters, the people I talk to every day are merely housed in the seed of their future body.

At the revelation of the glory of God's children, all of creation will marvel. Giant sequoias will stand in awe when they behold the resurrection bodies of the once frail and weak men who stood in their shadows. And each and every man will outlive not only the giant sequoias, but every star in the sky.

The fact that every man has eternity stamped in his genes is both bad news and good news. Eternity with God is one thing. Eternity in hell is another thing altogether. Can any of us deliver a man from hell? Of course not! We can no more accomplish that feat than we can raise the dead or heal the blind. Getting men off the path to hell and on their way to heaven requires God's help. Indeed, I think the situation is worse than that. I think we need God's help to make us care about the destiny of our friends. I suspect you know what I mean . . . don't you? With eternity at stake every day we obsess with work and sex and school and sex and recreation and sex and family and sex . . . well, you get the idea.

GOD HELPS US SEARCH

So how can God help us care enough to fulfill his intended purpose for our lives? Actually, we've got to go back to the vineyard and abide in Jesus. As we do so the helper will create in us the desire to fulfill God's purpose, which is "to seek and to save what was lost" (Luke 19:10). Those eight simple words form Christ's purpose statement for himself and for us.

Earlier in his ministry Jesus told three parables that communicated the intensity of his search. The first involved a shepherd looking for a lost sheep—which would be something like a man today looking for a lost dog. The second concerned a woman looking for a lost coin—which would parallel a woman today looking for a lost wedding ring. And the third, and most powerful, concerned a father constantly watching for his runaway son to return home (Luke 15). In each story the pursuit was intense and persistent—it didn't end until what was lost had been found. And in each story a great celebration followed the recovery.

I've got to confess I'm well acquainted with losing things. In fact, I'm going to form a national organization called Losers Anonymous. I recently bought the domain name. And as you may have guessed, this will be an exclusive club. Only certifiable "losers" will be allowed to join—they'll have to take a survey like the one that helps alcoholics determine if they're really drunks. Questions will include: Have family members ever expressed concern about how often you lose things? Have you lost five or more things in the last month? Do you ever lose things when alone? Have you missed school or work because you were looking for something like car keys? Have you ever said something you regret—like swearwords—while looking for a lost item?

Losers like me have to come up with some effective game plans for finding lost items. For instance, when I lose my car keys I have a proven strategy to locate them. First, I look in the key drawer. Second, I look in my pants. Third, I look in the ignition of the car. Fourth, I look under the driver's seat. Fifth, I look to the left of the driver's seat. Sixth, I look to the right of the passenger's seat. If the keys don't show up in any of those locations I repeat steps one through six over and over again until they're found. I hate to admit it, but on more than one occasion, after I've repeated those steps numerous times, my wife will stand by the key drawer, holding back a laugh while holding up my keys. "I found them in the key drawer," she'll say in a honey-sweet tone. After my wife's discovery, I may be a bit frustrated, but I'm also thrilled that my lost keys have been found and I can go on my way.

Have you ever noticed, though, that nobody celebrates when something is where it's supposed to be? Nobody ever pulls their keys off the key rack and informs everyone within shouting range, "I've found my keys! I've found my keys!" Do you wake up in the morning and celebrate that your watch hangs on your wrist or your car waits in the garage? Of course not! You only rejoice when you find a *lost* key or watch or car.

Jesus knew that we could all identify with the celebration following the successful end to an extensive search for a treasured item. And so he built a bridge between our experience and heaven. While we rejoice over a found key, Jesus said heaven celebrates whenever a lost man is found. In that moment angels high-five, pop confetti canisters, blow whistles, and turn loose balloons. Unseen to us, those same angels watched for years as God used guys like you and me to search for that lost man. And in the moment he's found, the angels know what we barely comprehend . . . that formerly lost and now found man has received forgiveness, hope, purpose, strength, and all of eternity with God.

TWO QUESTIONS

My first question is this: Why don't we actively share Christ's purpose? I suspect there are two reasons. First, we don't see the value of every man. Second, we don't feel the urgency of the search. But wait. Something about those last two sentences pulls me down into a dark place. Do you feel it too? After writing them I reread them several times trying to figure it out. And then I saw it. Those statements evoke feelings of guilt in me. I've felt it before when a well-intentioned preacher uttered them in an attempt to deepen my concern for my friends. But I haven't changed—not fundamentally.

And so I'm tempted to delete them and move on to a lighter point. But that won't work either, because they're the truth. We can't run away from truth because it exposes something in us that we already know is amiss . . . something we can't change. But isn't that precisely where God wants us? In a place where we must change to realize our purpose and yet in a place where we will never change without his help. Because of our bent toward indifference, we must ask God to help us care . . . to give us the heart of Christ.

Because of our bent toward indifference, we must ask God to help us care . . . to give us the heart of Christ.

We must deal with our guilt and sense of inadequacy, not by running away but by running to God. We must pray, and pray daily, that he will align our hearts with his and show us that the seed of eternity lives in each man. We must ask him to convince us that when we allow him to touch a life through us that life is changed forever. And that gives our own lives meaning and value, which will last long after the elements have rubbed our name from the gravestone and future generations have forgotten we ever lived.

I'm often slow to learn and quick to forget important lessons. It would help if I had a glass-encased seed of a giant sequoia to carry in my pocket. As I walk down the street, or ride in a plane, or shop at a hardware store, I could hold it in my grasp. And it would remind me that every man is but a seed of his future eternal glory. I think if I consistently reminded myself of this truth I would begin to see past a man's hair, eyes, ears, teeth, shirt, pants, shoes, coat, car, job, and house. I would see past his boasts and his barriers. I think in time I'd see him as he could one day be. And I'd realize all of heaven is watching and waiting to see if I'll allow God to reach out to him through me.

Yes, heaven is watching. And as the angels watch, I know one thing for certain . . . if in the future I care about my friend, it's because I'm daily asking for God's help.

But then I encounter the second question. *Is there a reason to hurry?* Honestly, I don't wake up every day with a sense of urgency. That's odd, because I always feel rushed when looking for any other lost item. In fact, I've actually articulated what I believe is the inviolable law of searching for anything lost. It goes like this: "The amount of time available to find a lost item is inversely proportionate to the time available."

Here's what I mean. Have you ever lost your car keys early in the morning and said, "Oh, don't sweat it. I don't need them until tonight. They'll turn up"? It never happens that way with me. No way! I only lose my keys when I'm already late for an important appointment. I only misplace my driver's license when I'm trying to get through security at an airport. When a hiker is lost in the mountains, the searchers don't have weeks to find him. They've only got a day or two. The uniformed search leader never comes on TV and says, "Not to worry. We won't even start searching for few days. We've got lots of time."

Now don't get me wrong. I'm not one of those guys who tries to motivate men to connect a friend to God by saying, "What if he dies tomorrow in a head-on car wreck? Or, what if he's charred in a plane crash? Or, what if he falls off a ladder and cracks his head open and lives the rest of his life in a vegetative state? You'll have lost your opportunity, and you'll have to live with that the rest of your life."

That's not what I'm getting at here. That kind of guilt is definitely unproductive. What I'm trying to say is that God is currently working in the lives of your friends, teeing them up for an encounter with you. When they're ready, God providentially gives each of us "moments" that are ripe with opportunity. It could be when a friend has suffered a loss, or after a victory, or on the golf course, or while bowling, or while watching a sporting event, or fishing—it could be anywhere at anytime. But when that moment arrives on the scene, we've got to be ready to gently and wisely offer the hope of Christ.

If we miss that teachable moment in a friend's life—now I don't want to sound pessimistic here—it may not happen again anytime soon, or ever.

God is currently working in the lives of your friends, teeing them up for an encounter with you.

Have you ever given up the search for a lost item, say your keys—yes, I keep coming back to them because I lose mine a lot—and one day you unexpectedly spot them in the back of the wrong drawer or sitting behind a book on a bookshelf? Instead of grabbing them, you say to yourself, "Oh, that's where they are. I'll get them later." And then later you can't remember where it was you saw them.

That's what I'm talking about here. When that key moment with our friend arrives and we have a chance to let God find a lost man through us, we've got to go for it. We must not wait.

Such readiness only occurs as we abide in Christ throughout

the day. Just as we asked God to help us see the seed of eternity in our friends, we must ask him to keep us always alert, ready to speak a word of life into a listening ear and open mind.

What seemed like a boulder to Sisyphus is only a pebble to God. We don't need to live a life of futility—we just need to daily break the law of independence and ask for his help.

For Discussion

1. Why do men hesitate to ask for help?

2. Where do men often look for significance?

3. Reflect on the statement "The search for significance ends not at a place but with a Person." How might living with this attitude affect your life?

4. Read Galatians 5:22-23. Which fruit of the Spirit do you most need Christ to produce in your life? Why?

5. Why do you need Christ to help you search for those who don't know him? How would you carry out such a search?

6. Have you ever sensed that God wanted to use you in the life of a friend or family member as he drew that person to himself? What happened?

BREAK THE RULE:

What is your plan to break the rule of independence and ask for help?

5

THE RULE OF RESTRAINT

NEVER LOSE YOUR COOL

*When it was almost time for the Jewish Passover, Jesus went up to
Jerusalem. In the temple courts he found men selling cattle, sheep and
doves, and others sitting at tables exchanging money. So he made a whip
out of cords, and drove all from the temple area, both sheep and cattle;
he scattered the coins of the money changers and overturned their tables.
To those who sold doves he said, "Get these out of here! How dare you
turn my Father's house into a market!"*

JOHN 2:13-16

Now that you know I'm a loser, I'm going to tell you about
the day I lost my cool. I left Portland at 6 a.m., which meant I
arrived at the airport at 5 a.m., which meant I climbed out of
bed at 3:30 a.m. I don't know about you, but at that hour my
mind moves about as fast as a glacier. Anyway, the plane took
me to DFW, where I caught a connecting flight to St. Louis. The
American Airlines jet landed safely, I grabbed my bags, rented
a car, and headed for my hotel. By the time I checked in, it was
5 p.m. and I had just enough time to grab a bite to eat before
my 7 p.m. speaking engagement.

At that moment my anger thermostat read sixty-eight
degrees. That's where I normally keep it. I was hungry and
eager to enjoy some food. The hostess seated me and left me

with a menu. A moment later the food server appeared—a twentysomething girl with short brown hair, bright blue eyes, a painted smile, and an attitude that told me, *Make it fast, buster.*

"Could you tell me what's the best meat item on the menu?" I asked. My question flowed from the fact that a few years earlier my doctor had told me, in a tone as serious as a mortician's, to go on a low-carb diet.

The waitress lifted her nose high and smugly said, "I don't know. I'm a vegetarian."

In that moment I lost my cool. With a single sentence she had opened a door that allowed a blast of hot emotions to overwhelm my cooling system. I wasn't as hot as a smelting furnace or even a sauna. Though I wasn't about to explode, I felt a compulsion to right a wrong that had been committed against me. Now don't get me wrong. I don't have anything against vegetarians. Honestly. It's just that she somehow communicated that she felt morally superior to me since she ate plants and I would eat the likes of Bambi the deer, Elsie the Cow, Roger the Rabbit, or Donald the Duck . . . pass on Mickey the Mouse.

"How can you eat plants with a clear conscience?" I asked.

"What do you mean?"

"Aren't you aware that all plant life exists on a conscious level?"

"That's ridiculous," she said.

"No. It's true. If you don't believe me go to www.plantscream. com, and you can hear a streaming audio of wheat creatures screaming out in agony as they're cut down by a combine."

"Right," she said—with a nasal tone that said, "I'm still better than you."

"I'd like to know how you can eat a slice of bread knowing that hundreds of wheat people were slaughtered so they could be turned into a loaf of bread sold at Safeway."

"Well, how can you eat a steak?" she asked.

I paused and contemplated her question. "It's hard," I said. "But at least only one cow died so I could eat that steak. And that dead cow will feed a lot of people. When you eat a slice of bread it has cost the lives of who knows how many wheat creatures. What bothers me is that in order to sustain itself that cow probably ate millions of grass people over the course of its life."

Hoping to silence me, the frustrated waitress turned to a young man at her side. I suspect he was a waiter in training. "Isn't that the craziest thing you've ever heard?" she asked.

Instead of offering her a lifeline he threw her an anchor. "No. It's true," he said. "I've been to the Web site. You should check it out."

Frustrated, she stomped off as the two of us laughed and high-fived.

That brief interchange was a sarcastic expression of anger intended to even the score for a perceived put-down. And it pales when compared to the name-calling, fist throwing, finger flipping, car swerving, knife wielding, and gun shooting that occurs every day in homes, on freeways, in schools, and places of employment. Because unbridled anger has the same dangerous potential of live ammunition thrown into a fire, men are often taught that the best way to control anger is to never get mad. Of course, telling a man not to get mad works about as well as telling an upset woman not to cry. But still . . . many men live with the notion that all anger is wrong and that they're spiritually unfit, since they get mad.

In this chapter I'm going to tell you why it's okay to break the rule of restraint and lose your cool—as long as you never lose control. And beware . . . I'm not suggesting it's ever okay to verbally or physically brutalize someone in an angry outburst. Nor am I recommending that you stuff your anger and suffocate someone with silence or sarcasm. What I'm saying is that it's not wrong for your emotional temperature to rise. In fact, there are occasions and situations that should stir up your anger.

Because unbridled anger has the dangerous potential of live ammunition thrown into a fire, men are often taught that the best way to control anger is to never get mad.

UNDERSTANDING ANGER

Webster's tells us the word *anger* means an intense emotional state induced by displeasure.[10] That's a good starting place, but we all know that anger involves more than just our emotions. We get mad because an event triggers our anger—like that guy who cut me off on the freeway yesterday. I lost my cool fast when he swerved into my lane. As my temperature rose, adrenaline rushed through my body, my heart rate increased, my blood pressure rose, and I felt like camping on my horn or racing ahead and cutting him off. Anger never discriminates, it involves the entire man—body, mind, emotions, and will.

The Source of Anger

Where does such a powerful emotion come from? Actually, it's a gift from God. In his excellent book *The Other Side of Love*, Gary Chapman notes that, while anger is not an essential part of

God's nature, it flows "from two aspects of God's divine nature: God's holiness and God's love."[11] The word *anger* is used 455 times in the Old Testament, and in 375 of those instances God is the angry one. Whenever God observes the destructive results of man's sin, he gets mad. Why? Chapman puts it this way: "It is God's concern for justice and righteousness (both of which grow out of His holiness and love) that stimulates God's anger. Thus when God sees evil, God experiences anger. Anger is His logical response to injustice or unrighteousness."[12]

> *"When God sees evil, God experiences anger. Anger is His logical response to injustice or unrighteousness."*
>
> GARY CHAPMAN

Now here's how we fit into the big picture. Because God created us in his image, it's logical that we also have a concern for justice and rightness. "Anger, then, is the emotion that arises whenever we encounter what we perceive to be wrong."[13] A bit later in this chapter, we'll see what righteous anger looks like, as we look closer at Jesus' reaction to the money changers in the Temple.

What Makes You Mad?

Recently I sent an e-mail to over three thousand men and asked a single question: What three things make you mad? Over two hundred men responded, and I continued to get e-mails weeks later. While it wasn't a scientific survey, some of the results are supported by a professional survey conducted by Chuck Cowan at Analytical Focus, the former chief of survey design at the U.S. Census Bureau, and Cindy Ford and the survey team at Decision Analyst. They surveyed four hundred men for Shaunti Feldhahn, author of the book *For Women Only*. The bottom line of their survey and mine: Men place respect at the top of their hierarchy of needs. The results from my survey are shown in the graph below.

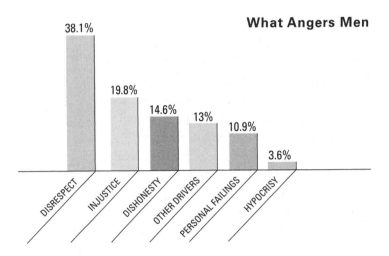

What Angers Men

It makes sense then, that if a man feels like he's being disrespected he will become angry. The perceived disrespect can be as seemingly innocent as a waitress implying a vegetarian is morally superior to a carnivore or as blatant as a wife questioning the honesty of her husband in the presence of his boss. Of course, anger triggered by feelings of disrespect isn't automatically appropriate. Before we discuss the times when we should break the rule of restraint, let's acknowledge the situations when reacting in anger is unwise.

REAL OR PERCEIVED WRONG

A few days ago at the gym where I work out, I spotted a middle-aged man with socks pulled up to his knees, tie-dyed shorts, and a T-shirt that said, "What Happens in Vegas, Stays in Vegas." As he sat at a pull-down machine that's designed to strengthen the back, a younger guy with short black hair and a shorter fuse approached him. Red-faced, the young man asked, "Didn't you see me sitting there next to the machine?"

"No, I didn't," he said as he pulled the handles down.

"I was sitting right there. How could you not have seen me?"

"I didn't see you. But what's the big deal? There's another machine just like this one," he said as he pointed to another machine less than ten feet away. "Use it."

The moment I saw that interchange I knew that the angry man felt disrespected. Someone had failed to honor his place in line.

Men feel disrespected when their wives are late, when they get poor service, and when they get turned down for sex. But based on what I've witnessed on the highway, nothing seems to make men angrier than when another driver disregards their space or right to the passing lane on a freeway. One man said, "I'm mild mannered by day. But put me behind the wheel of a four-thousand-pound vehicle and I become a maniac, angry at every person on the road who doesn't drive as aggressively as me."

Our problem is we often get angry about a "perceived" wrong rather than a "legitimate" wrong.

In addition to getting mad about perceived wrongs, another factor can compound the problem some of us have with anger. While I tend to keep my anger thermostat at around sixty-eight degrees, I know men whose thermostat is stuck at around ninety degrees. Why? Because over the years when they've been disrespected or treated unjustly, they didn't process their anger properly. So instead of going away, it's built up. A man like that only needs a spark of disrespect to ignite an explosion of rage.

Sometimes even the coolest man will find his thermostat stuck in a high position. That happens when he's had a series of disappointments or failures at work or home that lower his sense of self-respect and raise his internal temperature. A normally calm and patient man will suddenly lash out at his kids for an offense that he overlooked the day before.

CONTROLLING YOUR TEMPERATURE BY LEARNING TO LISTEN

Too often we become like Don Quixote, the hero of Cervantes' 1605 Spanish novel, whose vivid imagination blinded him to reality. He believed windmills stood as giants, flocks of sheep moved as armies, and galley slaves worked as oppressed gents. Similarly, we react to perceived wrongs that are not really wrongs at all. We internalize our anger or we swear and honk, fuming over imaginary words of disrespect. We kick machines that intend us no harm.

Isn't that what Cain did? When God accepted Abel's animal sacrifice and rejected Cain's grain offering, Cain got mad. He believed God had treated him unjustly. Rather than listening to God's advice and dealing with his own sin, Cain nursed his unjustified anger until it grew into a seething rage. He then murdered his brother.

We don't want to live like Don Quixote or Cain. We will lose our cool, some of us more than others, but it's crucial we get angry for a just cause. And it's equally important that if we're angry because of a "perceived" wrong or an irritation, we recognize it and quickly cool off. One way to do that is to listen. When someone or something stirs your anger, don't react—investigate. Listen. Learn.

It was James, the half brother of Jesus, who wrote: "This you know, my beloved brethren. But everyone must be quick to hear, slow to speak and slow to anger; for the anger of man does not achieve the righteousness of God" (James 1:19-20, NASB).

The original recipients of James's letter felt the sting of persecution. As Hebrew Christians they suffered at the hands of their fellow Jews who rejected Christ as the Messiah. They suffered greatly and they suffered unjustly. Yet James, their pastor, writing to his persecuted friends, urged them to cool the rising temperature of their anger by listening . . . and getting all the facts.

THAT WAS STUPID!

I did something when I was only six that I've never forgotten. My dad had given me a rocket for my birthday. The picture on the box top promised it would fly high with a puff of smoke and a trail of sparks. But it had to be assembled, and I couldn't read the instructions. And even if I could, I knew I'd never successfully put it together—there were just too many parts.

Day after day I begged my dad to assemble it for me. As he delayed the launch date, my anger heated up. After a week or two my anger turned into a seething rage. One day I took the box that contained the rocket into a room at the back of the garage. I removed the top of the box and stared at the unassembled parts. I snapped. In an outpouring of six-year-old rage, I ripped the rocket apart. I threw sections of it against the wall. I crushed the motor, side fins, and fuselage under my shoe.

When I had vented my wrath, I looked at what I had done.

While I was only a boy, I learned an important life lesson that I've never forgotten: *That was stupid.* I knew that in my fit of rage I had destroyed something that could not be repaired. And I decided that I'd never make that mistake again. Over the years I've been surprised at how that childhood moment has motivated me to pause before expressing my anger.

Looking back, I wish I had known enough to sit down with my dad and ask him why he hadn't been able to assemble the rocket. I suspect he would have given me a number of good reasons. Maybe it would have taken several hours and he needed to wait until he knew we could start the project and finish it. Perhaps I would have learned that we needed to take it out of town to launch it, which would have taken an entire day. I suspect he might have even given me a specific date that I could have then looked forward to. One thing I'm sure of—my anger was unjustified. And even if he had shown me some disrespect, it didn't justify my destructive outburst that kept that rocket forever on the ground.

I use that childhood illustration because what a child lacks, you and I possess. We have the thinking and reasoning ability to sort through our thoughts and feelings. We're able to ask questions to determine if our anger is triggered by a real or perceived injustice.

So when you break the rule of restraint and lose your cool—listen. Ask yourself, *Why am I mad? Is my anger justified? Did someone intentionally disrespect me? Am I responding to an injustice done to others? Am I reacting to a miniature wrong as though it was a massive wrong because of pent-up anger that I haven't processed properly?*

If it's appropriate, and you can do so graciously, talk with the person or persons who triggered your anger. You may discover that no offense was intended. They may give you a valid reason for their behavior.

I'M MAD, AND I'M NOT GOING TO TAKE IT ANYMORE . . .

While reacting in anger to a perceived wrong or because of pent-up frustration is foolish, anger does have its place. In my informal survey, I found that men get mad when they see someone with power take advantage of those with no power. They gave examples of favoritism at work, racism, and abortion. Dishonesty, personal failings, and hypocrisy also make men angry.

In each of those instances a wrong of some kind triggers anger. As followers of Christ we should get mad about the killing of unborn children, and the burning of African-American churches by racists, and religious leaders abusing those under their care, and the empty stomachs of starving children in much of the world. These are the kinds of things that should stir up our anger, not the petty wrongs we encounter every day. Consider the well-thought-out anger of the rock star Bono. He's consistently expressed anger that Americans—in particular Christian Americans—ignored the AIDS pandemic for so long. For the best picture of how righteous anger should be expressed in everyday life, though, we need look no further than to Christ.

Jesus was thirty years old when he first cleansed the Temple. It occurred to me that he had probably visited the Temple during every Passover celebration since he was age twelve. If so, he had repeatedly smelled the steaming dung and heard the cacophony of mooing, bleating, and shouting that accompanied the calls of the merchants and money changers in the Temple.

Because the only "clean" money was Jewish money, people with foreign currency had to exchange it before buying animals they could present as an offering to God. And then there were the animals. Those selling them took advantage of the buyers with excessively high prices. But what may have most angered Jesus was the fact that all of this happened in the Court of the Gentiles—the only place where non-Jews could come to pray and worship God. Instead of creating a quiet place of prayer, the Jews had turned it into a loud and smelly marketplace.

I'd guess that each time Jesus entered the Court of the Gentiles, the scene stoked his anger. Yet he waited for years before saying anything. During his younger years, Jesus must have gathered information and processed his anger with his Father.

When he finally expressed his indignation, he fully understood the injustice suffered by the worshippers and the disrespect shown to his Father's house. Jesus enters the Temple, where he grabs pieces of rope, loose tethers, and baggage cords that lay strewn about, plaiting them into a rope. Without warning he swings the whip, hitting a cow on the rump and moving it and the rest of the cows out of the Temple. Then he drives out the sheep and oxen and their owners. After that he pours out the coins of the money changers, flips over their tables, and forces the stunned men out. To those selling doves, he says, "Get these out of here! How dare you turn my Father's house into a market!" (John 2:16).

I'm impressed that Jesus never lost control of himself, even in the heat of anger. He expressed his anger without sinning. He even demonstrated restraint by not releasing the doves. All of the animals could be rounded up and the money scooped up. But if he had released the doves they would have flown away, causing loss to their owners.

Jesus' anger propelled him to right a wrong. But his actions weren't knee-jerk. Nor should ours be. It always makes sense to remember the words of Solomon: "A gentle answer turns away wrath, but a harsh word stirs up anger" (Proverbs 15:1). Harsh words often show disrespect toward the hearer and stoke their anger. A wise person may lose his cool, but he's careful how he expresses himself.

When angry, it's usually, if not always, a good idea *not* to act on your initial impulse. Swallow your words. If necessary, walk away. Take time to allow God to help you process your anger.

A few months ago a friend said something that angered me. I immediately wrote a scathing response. And it felt good . . . real good. I savored the wound my words would inflict.

When angry, it's usually a good idea not *to act on your initial impulse.*

But I didn't send it. Instead, I ran it past my wife and a friend. I rewrote it numerous times. Finally, when the rough edges were sanded away and my anger had subsided, I sent a very different and redemptive message. A few days later my friend called, and a healthy and healing conversation followed.

The outcome would have been different if I had sent the first flaming draft. We all need to thoughtfully process and communicate our anger. Nobody understood this better than Solomon. He said, "A fool gives full vent to his anger, but a wise man keeps himself under control" (Proverbs 29:11). Losing your cool doesn't mean losing control. Don't ever express your anger until you're prepared to do so wisely.

Of course, when you suffer disrespect or injustice, you won't always have several days to process your anger and develop a healthy response. Your wife may say something that stings. Your kids may smart-off disrespectfully. Or someone may cut you off on the freeway. Even then . . . don't act on your initial impulse. Ask yourself why you're angry. Consider whether it was a wrong or a perceived wrong. If you can't act with grace . . . walk or drive away.

Behind all of this is a crucial spiritual truth that underlies why you should be quick to hear, slow to speak, and slow to anger.

CONTROL YOUR TEMPERATURE BY REMEMBERING GOD

The apostle James said, "The anger of man does not achieve the righteousness of God" (James 1:20, NASB). God's anger is always justified and is always expressed perfectly. Why? Because he's able to determine, without error, when a wrong has been committed. God never gets angry about a *perceived* injustice. He never flies off the handle because of an imaginary evil. We, on the other hand, do that all the time. In fact, I suspect we bristle at perceived wrongs or irritations far more often than we do at real ones. I know I do. And that's why we should lose our cool slowly—our sense of justice never achieves the rightness of God's.

God never gets angry about a perceived injustice.

When we look at Jesus, we find that even when wronged, he seldom got angry. Four instances where he got mad stand out to me—the two cleansings of the Temple at the beginning and end of his ministry (John 2:13-25; Matthew 21:12-17), the time when the disciples prevented the children from coming to him (Mark 10:13-14), and the Sabbath when the religious leaders indicated it was unlawful for him to heal on that day (Matthew 12:9-14; Mark 3:5).

The Greek word used in Mark 10:14 indicates Jesus felt "indignation" toward the disciples. When Mark describes how Jesus looked at the Pharisees with "anger," he used a different word, *orge*, which refers to anger as the strongest of all passions.[14] Make no mistake, Jesus lost his cool and felt intense anger toward the hard-hearted Pharisees. Yet, in that same verse Mark notes that he felt "sympathy" or "grief" for the religious leaders.

I'm curious: When you're mad, how often do you feel compassion for the person you think wronged you? If you're like me, that happens about as often as you breathe underwater. I'm sure Jesus' compassion tempered his anger—he genuinely understood and cared for the people who repeatedly disrespected and injured others.

But there's another reason why Jesus maintained his cool. In 1 Peter 2:23 we read, "When they hurled their insults at him, he did not retaliate; when he suffered, he made no threats. Instead, he entrusted himself to him who judges justly."

Instead of threatening those who crucified and mocked him, Jesus trusted his Father to right any wrongs. Too often men get angry because of insignificant wrongs. In those moments, we feel like the guy at the gym and take it upon ourselves to confront the offender. Like the thoughtless guy:

- ▶ who darts into the parking spot you have been waiting for
- ▶ who unloads twenty items at the nine-item checkout line

- ▶ who closes the restaurant ten minutes early and won't let you eat even though your family has driven across town to make it *before* ten
- ▶ who talks in the theater
- ▶ who drives slowly in the left lane of a freeway

All these, and an endless list of similar offenses, are petty and irrelevant. And even the big-time offenses we suffer could often best be handled by walking away and letting God set things right. But whether we walk away or confront someone, we need to process our anger quickly. Paul said we shouldn't even let the sun set on it. Why? Because unprocessed anger doesn't just go away. Like smallpox, it spreads with a deadly force. It infects our mind with bitterness, rage, and hatred and then infects others. The devil delights in using our ill will to accomplish his evil ends (see Ephesians 4:27-28).

All of this puts us in a tight spot. I see clearly that anger requires maturity to manage. We can lose our cool, but not control—which is easier for some men to say than to do. However, these are some steps we can take when we feel anger welling up:

- ▶ We need to listen and seek understanding.
- ▶ We need to determine whether the wrong was real or perceived.
- ▶ We need to avoid acting on our initial impulse.
- ▶ We need to be slow to speak—expressing our anger only after we've processed it and can speak and act redemptively.

▶ In most cases we simply need to allow God to right any wrong.

Considering that this is a book about breaking rules, it may seem odd that I just gave you five steps for losing your cool without losing control. The moment I think managing anger is about keeping rules, I'm doomed to failure. Yet Scripture gives us clear direction on how to respond when we get angry. As we abide in him, Jesus will use our indignation to accomplish his purpose through us. As Gary Chapman observes:

> Our anger is at the very heart of who we are. Tell me what you are angry about and I will tell you what is important to you. For the mature Christian, anger will focus on true injustice, unfairness, inequity, and ungodliness; not on petty personal irritations. For the mature Christian such anger will motivate positive efforts to establish justice, fairness, equity, and godliness. His anger will be tempered with mercy and humility realizing that he too is capable of falling. To use the words of the ancient Hebrew prophet, "He has showed you, O man, what is good. And what does the Lord require of you? To act justly and to love mercy and to walk humbly with your God" (Micah 6:8).[15]

For Discussion

1. What one situation most often makes you mad?

2. How do you usually process and express anger?

3. Why should you be slow to anger?

4. In what types of situations does our getting angry reflect God's image?

5. What should make you mad? Does it? Why or why not?

6. How does your focus differ when you express appropriate or righteous anger compared to when you express inappropriate or sinful anger? What motivates righteous anger versus sinful anger?

7. What can we learn about appropriate anger from Jesus' response to the money changers in the Temple?

8. Can you describe a time in your life when you perceived an injustice being done and then reacted with righteous anger? What was the result?

9. How will abiding in Christ help you process and express anger? Write out the specific steps that will help you lose your cool without losing control.

BREAK THE RULE:

When will you break the rule of restraint
and lose your cool?

6

THE RULE OF IMPRESSING OTHERS

NEVER LOOK STUPID

During the fourth watch of the night Jesus went out to them, walking
on the lake. When the disciples saw him walking on the lake, they were
terrified. "It's a ghost," they said, and cried out in fear.
But Jesus immediately said to them: "Take courage!
It is I. Don't be afraid."
"Lord, if it's you," Peter replied, "tell me to come to you on the water."
"Come," he said.
Then Peter got down out of the boat, walked on
the water and came toward Jesus.

MATTHEW 14:25-29

I pulled our Pathfinder into the garage and there stood my wife—waiting for me. Before I could exit the car, she told me someone at Costco had called to say I had left my planner there. Apart from the fact that it contained my driver's license, credit cards, PalmPilot, and three dollars in cash—it had no value.

Frustrated, I retraced the route I had just completed and returned to Costco. The smiling customer service rep pulled my planner from a drawer and asked if I had any ID. I told her it was in the planner. As she checked to make sure I was the same guy as the one pictured on my driver's license, I told her, "I was doing so well. I've been on the wagon for six months."

"And that means?" she asked.

"I'm a member of Losers Anonymous, and I haven't lost any-thing for six months."

"What's Losers Anonymous?" she asked.

I proceeded to tell her all about the national organization and how it had helped many people, including me, live free of our disease.

To my right stood a woman in her sixties with grayish blue, Marine-short hair. She wore stylish Southwestern garb and a ton of turquoise jewelry around her neck, her wrists, her fin-gers, and hanging from her earlobes. She also wore a fashion-able tan leather jacket with fringe on the sleeves and shoulders. She looked like she had just returned from Santa Fe.

She listened intently as I told the clerk that the first thing every morning I stand in front of a mirror and say, "I'm Bill. I'm a loser."

The clerk knew I was joking, but the chic dresser took me seriously. "That's terrible," she said. "You should never speak that way about yourself. I'd encourage you to get out of that organization immediately."

With the seriousness of a bomb-squad member, I said, "The first step in overcoming the disease is to admit my failing. I must embrace the truth about myself. That . . . I'm a loser."

"That's terrible," she said, "just terrible."

"It's necessary," I said as I took my planner and left. Five min-utes later I realized I had left my cell phone at Costco. I turned around and returned a second time. As I approached the cus-tomer service counter, the clerk held up my phone and said, "Loser!"

The first loss was funny. The second one identified me as not only a loser, but stupid. When I say stupid, I mean one who is "slow to learn or understand. Tending to make poor decisions or careless mistakes . . . a foolish person."[16]

Now, since men place respect at the top of their hierarchy of needs, no man wants to be seen as stupid. I don't mind it when a customer service rep sees me as funny, witty, and entertaining. But I don't want to be viewed as stupid . . . a loser who never wins rather than someone who merely loses things.

Since men place respect at the top of their hierarchy of needs, no man wants to be seen as stupid.

Yeah, I know. I've met guys who say, "I don't care what anyone thinks of me." But I never believe them. Every man wants to be respected and looked up to. In fact, I think men exert considerable effort trying to keep the sixth rule: Impress others by attempting never to look stupid. The problem is that a man who lives by this rule will never take any chances. And a man who takes no chances isn't living, he's languishing. Jesus consistently violated the rule of impressing others. From a purely human perspective, a man who threatens to destroy the existing religious system, calls the reigning power brokers "whitewashed tombs," and professes to be God certainly isn't trying to win favor with the religious and political leaders of his day.

And in case you think he did all of this to win over the masses, think again. Remember, the crowd that hailed him as king one day cried for his death the next. Jesus lived to impress nobody but his Father. And he didn't care how foolish or unwise his behavior may have appeared; if it aligned with his Father's will, that's all that mattered.

But he was also teaching his disciples about the value of

breaking the law of impressing others. He showed them the importance of throwing popular opinion to the wind and behaving so radically they endangered their reputation. He warned them that following him could alienate family members and friends. They could be considered stupidly foolish instead of cautiously wise. Yet, as they followed Jesus, they would discover that only such radical living would allow them to serve as conduits of God's power. All others would live respected and boring and respected and mundane and respected and monotonous and respected and weary lives . . . respected for their prudent, cautious vanilla life and faith.

Given his exuberant nature, perhaps it's not surprising that the apostle Peter chose to break this rule in dramatic fashion. On the night—or early morning, depending on how you would describe 3 a.m.—that Peter broke the law of impressing others, all of the disciples were in a boat, in a gale, in darkness, in a state of exhaustion.

Talk about a change of circumstances. In a matter of hours they had gone from celebration to chaos. Just the day before Jesus had multiplied five loaves and two fish and used them to feed five thousand men. We're talking about a picnic of at least fifteen thousand people if you include the women and children. After that impressive miracle the throng concluded Jesus was the coming prophet and wanted to make him their king—no doubt an idea embraced by the disciples. Realizing this, Jesus dispersed the crowd, sent the disciples off in a boat, and climbed up a hill to pray.

When the disciples first entered the water, the Sea of Galilee looked as smooth as Lake Austin at sunrise. But after they had rowed too far from shore to turn back, a vicious storm hit the sea, turning it into a dark, rolling monster. The men strained at the oars but the wind held them steady like a strong anchor. I suspect Peter and the rest of the disciples wished they had never gotten into the boat. They must have had the same sinking feeling experienced by the lady on a plane in a turbulent storm. Trying to calm the distraught man sitting beside her, she said, "Sir, I'm sure the pilots have everything under control. You don't need to worry."

To which he replied: "Lady, I *am* a pilot. That's why I'm so worried."

But then again . . . *Jesus* had sent them to the other side of the Sea of Galilee.

Of course, their scary situation turned terrifying when the soaked disciples saw what they believed to be a ghost walking on the water. This was no scare caused by someone saying "Boo!" from behind a partially opened door or even the fright caused by a scene from *Psycho*, *Alien*, or *The Shining*. These men were fighting for their lives, and it appeared as if Death had walked across the sea to take them home.

That's when the ghost proved not to be a ghost at all, but Jesus. "Take courage!" he said. "It is I. Don't be afraid."

As surprised as they were at the sudden and unexpected appearance of Jesus, the speed with which Peter asked his question may have surprised them even more. "Lord, if it's you," Peter replied, "tell me to come to you on the water."

Jesus spoke a single word in response. "Come."

While we can't know for certain what went through Peter's mind, I think in that moment he knew if Jesus said, "Come," nothing else in life mattered. Certainly not the possibility that he could fall into the water and look like a fool. Or even the likelihood that the other disciples would view him as dangerously impulsive. When a man has a once-in-a-lifetime chance to walk on water, should he care if others think he's stupid?

In that moment Peter knew if Jesus said, "Come," nothing else in life mattered.

So when is the right time to break the law of impressing others? I'd suggest the time is right when you face the following four conditions.

CONDITION ONE: YOU'RE IN A BOAT

As a high school student I'd get up at 5 a.m., toss my ski across the backseat of my black and white '57 Pontiac, drive to Westlake Dock, climb in our boat with a buddy, and hit Lake Austin just as the yellow ball touched the horizon with a sizzling heat. The boat would skim across the glass-smooth water and I'd barefoot behind it—each foot throwing up a six-foot rooster tail. Now that I'm a scuba diver I've got different boating experiences. I load my gear on to the dive-boat and kick back as the captain takes us to a reef that hides below crystal-clear water.

Unlike me, Peter, a professional fisherman, didn't view boats as recreational toys. I doubt he ever took someone on a sight-seeing tour of the Sea of Galilee, although I suspect his boat was big enough. The largest boats on the Sea of Galilee were 26½ feet long, 7½ feet wide, and 4½ feet high with four rowers and as many as nine riders. While that boat might not hold too many people today, back then the average man only stood five feet five inches tall and weighed about 140 pounds.

Peter began the night on which he took his water walk in familiar surroundings. And as the storm raged around him, only his wooden boat protected Peter from the water and sheltered him from the storm. It provided a setting that maximized his training and experience as a fisherman. And if he had let it, the boat could have been a barrier between Peter and the miraculous power of God.

As you've likely guessed . . . we've all got a boat. Author and pastor John Ortberg noted that our boat is anything that represents safety and security apart from God himself. It's whatever produces fear when we think of leaving it behind.[17] Your boat could be your job, a relationship, a home, a car, a recreational activity, a compulsive or addictive behavior, or the approval of your spouse or boss.

If you want to stretch your faith and grow spiritually, you'll have to climb out of the boat and step onto the water. Yeah, I know it's scary. That's how I felt when I stepped out of my boat five years ago and walked away from my job as a pastor to launch a national men's ministry. I hoped the water would provide strong support for my feet, but I wasn't sure. I thought I might look stupid—especially if I lost my house and had to live with my wife under a bridge in Portland. But I possessed confidence that God wanted me to get out of my boat—and so I did.

A week after taking that first fearful step, I addressed a church in Anchorage, Alaska. I told the story of David's mighty men and how I believed today, as then, God wants men who will fight for right, fight for their families, fight through pain, and fight for a strong faith.

Afterward, a man approached me and said, "My name's Brett. Does your ministry have a Web site?"

"No, we don't. We've only been going a week."

"I own a company and a number of Web designers work for me. I'd like to build your site."

"Great. But I don't have any money."

"Even if you did, I'd do it for free. I believe in your message. Men need to hear it." Over the next couple of months his designers built and launched http://www. millionmightymen.com and http://www.millionprayingwomen.com.

One week after I returned from Alaska I was speaking at a men's breakfast in Canby, Oregon. After giving the message about David's mighty men, a dark-haired man with a slim build and a great smile introduced himself as Rick Salz. He asked if my ministry had a logo, hats, and T-shirts. I told him that I didn't even have a business card.

"My company designs logos for companies, and we sell apparel with company logos and slogans on them. I want to do all of that for your ministry."

I appreciated his interest in my ministry but knew I couldn't afford his services. He saw my hesitation and said, "Of course, I'll do all of this without charge."

A few weeks later we had a logo, cool baseball hats, T-shirts, jackets, mugs—and just about anything else a guy would want.

Why had these two strangers approached me like that? I'm convinced God was working behind the scenes to let me know I hadn't made a mistake when I climbed out of the boat. He wanted to assure me that the water would hold if I'd just keep looking to him.

If you struggle with such fear in an area of your life, perhaps you've identified your boat. Maybe it's time to consider climbing out. But don't step onto the water yet. Remember—Peter didn't walk on the water as soon as he got into the boat. Two more conditions were present then and they must be for you too. And by the way . . . once you get out of the boat you'll encounter a fourth condition.

CONDITION TWO: GOD SENDS YOU INTO A STORM

Often when we set out on a voyage in pursuit of a God-given vision we expect smooth sailing. I suspect the disciples thought they'd be across the lake in a few hours. Unfortunately, it usually doesn't work like that. No, that's not true. It *never* works out that way.

Consider:

- ▶ Abraham and the delayed fulfillment of God's promise
- ▶ Joseph and his brothers' hatred leading to his imprisonment in Egypt
- ▶ Moses and the resistance of Pharaoh and the rebellion of the Jews
- ▶ David and the jealous rage of Saul and the years of running and hiding
- ▶ Elijah and the wrath of Jezebel

I could go on, but you get the idea. God gave each of those men a vision and then sent them into a storm. Just as he'll do with you.

I remember when my wife and I were celebrating our thirteenth wedding anniversary. As we enjoyed a delicious dinner at a romantic restaurant she said, "Well, honey, we've had twelve years of happy marriage."

Normally my wife is pretty accurate with things like birth dates and anniversaries, so I was surprised at her miscalculation.

Proud that I knew how long we had been married, and she had momentarily forgotten, I said, "It's been thirteen years."

Cindy smiled and tilted her head to one side. "I didn't think the first year was happy," she said.

Her words brought back one of the more painful memories of our relationship. We were still newlyweds who'd only been married six months when in the heat of an argument she said, "You're a lazy bum."

"And you're Porky Pig," I spat back.

Her words hit home.

Mine hit a nerve.

I slammed the front door, stomped down the stairs, jogged across the parking lot behind our apartment and climbed inside our high-powered V-8 Chrysler. After starting the engine, I floored the accelerator. The rear tires screamed as a cloud of black smoke billowed behind the car, filling the air with the stench of burning rubber and painting a black stripe on the asphalt.

Inside, Cindy struck back with a vengeance—she hid my socks.

When I returned home, several hours later, neither of us apologized. Instead, we pretended the other wasn't there. Our relationship couldn't have been colder if we'd been sitting on a block of ice in the North Atlantic.

Knowing it would snag her like a rusty hook, I turned on the television and kicked back in a comfortable chair. Ignoring me, she left for school.

When she returned home, I didn't exactly greet her with the warmth of a black lab. Need I mention—things had gotten bad.

No way could we have seen this coming. We had met two years earlier in Dallas and fallen in love. I attended school at the University of Texas in Austin. Cindy attended Southern Methodist University in Dallas. Countless nights after finishing my shift as a waiter, I'd make the two-hundred-mile drive north to Dallas. After a year of this long-distance relationship, she transferred to UT so we could spend more time together.

Not everyone approved of our courtship. Her parents sniffed something foul in the relationship. Or, more precisely, in me. "He's not Jesus," her dad once told Cindy. Seeing her infatuation with me, he cautioned: "Nobody's perfect."

And while I knew Cindy had some flaws, my knowledge was theoretical. She seemed as close to perfect as I'd ever find in a girl.

Not wanting to take any chances, we attended premarital counseling sessions with our pastor. Of course, we realized other couples, less in love, less communicative, less passionate, and less spiritual, encountered all sorts of marital hurdles. And so we listened and learned and felt more than ready.

Nothing had prepared us for the relational toxin in which we were marinating the night of our big fight.

That night, after we had each climbed into bed, repelling each other like the negative ends of two magnets, I asked Cindy, "Would you marry me again?"

Before her heart could beat she said, "No way!"

"Would you marry me again?" she asked.

"Not a chance," I said.

We had reached the proverbial bottom of the barrel and weren't even looking up. The words of Simon and Garfunkel's 1964 song might have been penned by either of us that night:

"Hello darkness, my old friend." I can't remember a darker place in our marriage. Or a more helpless and hopeless feeling.

"Seems like we've got no one to turn to but God."

"Seems that way," Cindy whispered.

What happened next is as impossible to describe as the fragrance of rain on freshly cut grass. I know the smell. But I can't capture the scent inside a bottle of words so you can unscrew the lid and enjoy the fragrance. On that night God bent down and touched our marriage in a profound way. And we've never recovered.

It began with a prayer. So many years have passed that I can't recall the exact words. But it went something like this: "God, we are hopelessly and helplessly caught up in our own selfishness and anger. Apart from your grace, our lives and marriage are doomed. Please save our marriage."

In that moment the knots in our soul were suddenly severed, emotional tethers snapped, and we were free of the evil that had bound us. We embraced and wept deeply.

The next day we talked about how we had arrived at such a bad place. We each concluded the greatest shock and disappointment of marriage found its orbit, not around the other person's flaws, but around our own. We knew from that night on that God would not only let us sail into relational storms, he would get us through to the other side.

When it comes to entering new storms, I'm not alone. Just about every week I get an e-mail or call from a man who's in the middle of a storm into which God has led him. Most often it involves a problem at work—like a failing business, a broken promise, an uncertain future—or a relational crisis. If you're in a boat adrift in a storm, it may be time to break the rule of impressing others and step onto the water. But not yet. Before you climb over the edge, see if the third condition Peter encountered is there for you.

CONDITION THREE: GOD CALLS YOU TO SHARE IN THE SUPERNATURAL

In the summer of—gulp—1965, I was sixteen and having fun waterskiing and taking life easy. Sonny and Cher were together and singing "I've Got You Babe," and the number one song for the year was "Help," by the Beatles. My only problem involved my dad. He seemed to think that since he provided me with a boat and car, I should at least get a job and pay for the gas. So I got my first "man job" working for a moving company owned by a neighbor, Glenn Brown.

Early on that first Monday morning I showed up at the warehouse, and Mr. Brown introduced me to two other movers—Bevo and Rhino. These guys looked like NFL linemen who could have held night jobs as bouncers at a bar frequented by Hell's Angels. We drove to a palatial house on the lake and right away I established myself as a serious 140-pound player. I did that by lifting refrigerators, freezers, sofas, two-ton steel gun cases, and other heavy items onto my shoulders—well . . . maybe not that big and heavy.

About halfway through the job, Bevo called me aside. "Bill, everything in the house has to go. You're fast. How about if you load up all the small stuff, and Rhino and I will get the heavy furniture. We've found that it works best if big guys carry heavy stuff and little guys carry light stuff—that way nobody gets hurt."

I remember feeling good about his advice. Instead of commenting on my twiglike arms and bird legs and chest, he complimented my speed and importance to the team. At the end of the day I carried home some tired muscles and a few bruises. But I felt as proud as an Olympian wearing a gold medal. I had worked with men for the first time in my life. And I had gotten paid for my effort.

You probably remember your first job. That experience served as an important rite of passage. It signaled that you had moved from childhood to manhood. And it prepared you for your full-time vocation where you'd earn the money needed to support your family and buy the symbols of status—cars, homes, travel, and recreational toys.

But over time the thrill turns as boring as a job watching the second hand on a clock. The joy of a first job or a new job fades into a sense of meaninglessness. Ultimately, a man's career can't bring meaning to his life. That can only be accomplished by a call from God. It's the call of God that brings us from the boat into a supernatural experience.

Jesus spoke a single word to Peter: "Come." And he climbed out of the boat and stepped onto the water. The moment his foot touched the formerly-too-light-to-sustain-the-weight-of-a-man surface, it supported him as well as a frozen lake. But the lake wasn't frozen, and it didn't hold him because of a natural law—like water freezes at 32° Fahrenheit. It held him because Jesus exercised a power that overruled the laws of nature. Jesus changed the molecular structure of the water so it would hold Peter's weight, or he changed Peter so he could walk on the water. And as long as Peter focused on Christ and trusted in him, he moved as safely as a stroll on dry land. Peter experienced the supernatural when he stepped out of the boat and onto the water.

It's crucial for you to know that God has called you to do something that can only be accomplished by his power. His call will utilize your unique abilities and talents to expand his kingdom. But you'll never respond to his call if you're stuck in a boat and worried about taking a risk that could make you look foolish.

I'm not one of those guys who thinks the "call" of God involves an audible voice, usually in a melodious baritone like Charlton Heston, that gives you specific marching orders. Rather, it's a powerful mental and emotional urge to accomplish something that you couldn't do without God's power. The call will utilize all of your talents and resources to meet a specific need that has captured your heart. In other words, God's call to you will mesh with your passion.

I just returned from a two-week trip to India. I visited that ancient country to speak *and* to check out the possibility of becoming involved in working with orphans. Through an extraordinary series of circumstances that carried God's fingerprints and DNA, I hope to be involved in building an orphanage north of Mumbai. While I know that neither I nor those I influence can save every orphan, we can save some. We can touch one child who awakens every morning with empty hands, empty arms, empty hopes, and an empty heart.

Why did I make the trip to India? Because I believe God has called me to let some throwaway children know that God has heard their cries and his love is on the way.

I believe God has something special planned for you too . . . something that will make a difference in the world. Your call could involve feeding the poor, caring for orphans, building a church, discipling men, protecting the unborn, reaching a people group, or—well, you fill in the blank.

What is your call? Maybe you've almost forgotten it because so many years have passed since you received it. Or perhaps it's so bodacious you never took it seriously. It could be you need to ask God to extend a call—just like Peter did. If so, you'll need to ask every day until you hear his voice.

God's call will always draw you to Jesus. It will always involve risk. It will always evoke fear. It will always require God's power to get it done. And once you hear it you'll have to get out of your boat. That first step will be exhilarating. But beware—it will lead to the fourth condition.

> *God's call will always involve ristk. It will always envoke fear. It will always require God's power to get it done.*

CONDITION FOUR: YOUR FAITH IS TESTED

In taking those first steps, the fisherman passed the first test and seemed on his way to a successful water walk. And then the fear that had haunted him a few moments before when he thought Jesus was a ghost returned with the wind.

Peter's experience reminds me of the time I climbed the face of a steep ridge in Montana. I'm not a rock climber, so I don't do vertical cliffs, but this ridge was plenty steep. Anyway, I focused on my destination until I neared the summit. And then I made the mistake of looking down. The distance to the bottom of the ridge appeared much farther than it had when I was on the base of the ridge looking up. I realized that one false step would result in a rapid descent and almost certain death—or at least a broken neck, broken arms, broken legs, and a crushed skull.

I felt like wrapping my arms around a tree and calling for a helicopter to airlift me to safety. But there was no tree nearby or any means of communicating with the outside world. Besides, my friend had already scurried to the top and was waiting for me to follow. I made it to the summit, but not before overcoming a serious rush of fear turbocharged with an injection of adrenaline. Danger can paralyze any of us.

If not for the hazardous storm, Peter might have climbed back into the boat with dry sandals. He might have kept his focus if it had been a clear night with the light of a full moon reflecting off the water . . . just as I might have completed the climb without fear if I had been climbing a pitcher's mound. But it wasn't a clear, calm night.

The text says he "saw" the wind, which must mean, since wind is invisible, that he felt the force of the wind on his face and against his body and heard it stirring up the water. The wind distracted him from Jesus. He looked away and saw the waves rising and falling, the water blowing horizontally all around him, and Jesus' robe flapping furiously. In that moment Peter realized he was walking on water beyond the reach of the boat.

Fear took over and Matthew says he was beginning to sink. I find that last statement odd. Don't you? He didn't just sink. Instead he was "beginning" to sink. Maybe he sunk up to his ankles or knees. It must have been a strange sight, and I can't help but wonder what kept him from disappearing into the raging sea. Yet I think I know the answer. Peter only "began" to sink because, according to Jesus, he only "doubted." His fear didn't completely erode his faith.

But that fissure of doubt spread like an expanding crack on a windshield. Soon his faith shattered, and he felt his feet covered with water. In that moment he faced the second test of his faith: What would he do with his doubt?

Would he believe his doubt and sink, or gather up his courage and continue to walk on water? Would he leap for the boat? Would he try to swim to it? Or would he turn to Jesus and trust him to make up the gap between his faith and his doubt?

Of course, there's no surprise ending here. You know what happened. Peter called for help, and the Lord reached out a hand and restored his faltering faith. A moment later they both climbed into the boat. And then another miracle occurred— the wind died down. I can't avoid concluding that Jesus sent the wind to demonstrate his power—not only to test Peter's faith, but also to allow Peter to experience the rush of God's power.

I'm sure he does the same thing with us. The initial test involves getting out of the boat. Next we've got to trust Jesus to enable us to walk on water . . . to do something only he could empower us to do . . . something that involves risk and could make us look foolish, or downright stupid, if we go down.

Those are the first tests. The next one will occur when circumstances beyond our control blast away at our dream, creating doubts that feed our fear. We can believe our doubts and try to get back into the boat we just exited or frantically hunt for another one. Or, we can look to Jesus and trust him to keep us from sinking. This only happens as we abide in him. The more we know Christ, the more we'll trust him to enable us to walk on water even when the wind stirs up our doubts.

But wait a minute. None of this is possible unless we're willing to break the rule of impressing others. As we've seen, it's time to do that when the first three conditions converge:

- ▶ You're in a boat.
- ▶ God sends you into a storm.
- ▶ God calls you to share the supernatural.

The more we know Christ, the more we'll trust him to enable us to walk on water even when the wind stirs up our doubts.

Once these have taken place and you're walking on the water, expect the fourth condition:

- ▶ Your faith is tested.

While you're still in the boat, following the rule of impressing others leads to one of two responses: Either you'll stay in the boat because you fear looking stupid or you'll get out because you want to wow others. In either case, you're driven by self-serving motives. But there's a definite downside to either decision: People obsessed with impressing others fail to see or experience the power of God.

While Peter walked on water, many of Jesus' contemporaries lived devoid of God's supernatural power. John tells us many leaders who believed in Christ strictly obeyed the rule of impressing others. He said, "Because of the Pharisees they would not confess their faith for fear they would be put out of the synagogue; for they loved praise from men more than praise from God" (John 12:42-43). How tragic.

You see, don't you, that if I'm seeking to please others I've misplaced my faith. It's resting in myself and what I can do to win the applause of my audiences—including the enforcers of the add-on rules. The moment Peter "saw" the wind, his faith shifted from Christ to himself, and he doubted whether he could walk on the water . . . so he began to sink.

Let's get back to the importance of breaking this rule. If you want to walk on water you've got to determine that you'll live for the approval of God and no one else. Radical? Yes. But that's the kind of faith that prompts a man to step out of a boat . . . to call for help when he's "beginning" to sink. It's the only faith that will enable you to fulfill your God-given call and experience the Lord's great power.

For Discussion

1. What are some things men often do to impress others? What are some things you do to impress others?

2. Why do men try to avoid looking stupid? (Hint—remember the number one thing that makes men mad.)

3. What are some ways Jesus violated the rule of impressing others?

4. What's your boat?

5. What storms have you been in before? Are you in one now? If so, describe it.

6. In what way has God called you to share in the supernatural? Has he called you to fulfill a bodacious vision? If so, what is it?

7. Is it time for you to get out of your boat? Why or why not?

8. How has God tested your faith in the past? Is it being tested now? If so, how? How do you think God wants you to respond to the test?

BREAK THE RULE:

How will you break the rule of impressing others and look stupid?

AFTERTHOUGHTS

It occurred to me that you might find it hard to actually break the six rules discussed in this book. After all, it's normal to associate punishment with breaking rules. That's what life teaches us.

For instance, until recently I felt great pride because I had gone eighteen years without a single traffic ticket. I achieved this amazing record by paying close attention to the speed limit and my car's speedometer. In fact, to reward myself for always driving the speed limit, I bought a radar detector. Of course, I didn't buy it to warn me of a speed trap so I could slow down—since I never speed. Rather, whenever it would flash and beep, indicating the presence of a policeman with a radar gun, I'd look at my speedometer and smile—pleased that I was going the posted speed. In that way the radar detector served as a pat on the back—an "Attaboy" for my compliance with the law. As I would pass the speed trap, I'd wave and smile at the officer . . . we made a tight team.

You can imagine my shock, then, when a motorcycle cop pulled me over during rush-hour traffic. One thing I knew for sure, I wasn't speeding. Nobody was speeding. I figured maybe a brake light had burned out.

The cop parked behind me and approached my window. "Give me your driver's license, registration, and proof of insurance," he barked. It was a hot summer day, and I could tell he wasn't in a friendly mood. Not a good sign if I had committed a moving violation . . . an impossibility, I was sure, since I had spotted him a mile back.

As the cars, trucks, busses, and bikes swooshed by, stirring up dust and swirling around loose trash, the officer took my papers and walked to the rear of the car. Standing there, he opened his ticket ledger and began writing. I knew that a ticket is written in stone and cannot be unwritten. So unless he was writing me a warning, I would have no chance to invite him to join my team by helping me keep an unblemished driving record. Nor could I appeal to his sympathetic side by mentioning the fact that I was paying insurance for a family with three teenage boys, and I alone, with my perfect driving record, kept our car insurance payment lower than the national debt.

As those despairing thoughts filled my mind, he slapped shut his ledger, walked to my window, tore out the ticket, and handed it to me. That's when I noticed he wore a portable sauna—a helmet and black leather coat—someone once told me such clothes help keep a biker cool. He looked cool, but appeared hot. With everything going against me, I hoped that maybe, just maybe, in spite of the heat, traffic, and exhaust fumes, he nurtured a sense of humor.

"Is this an invitation to the annual police fund-raising circus?" I asked.

"No. It's a ticket. Pay it or challenge it in court."

He started to walk away when I asked, "What's it for?"

He looked at me and smile-snarled. "Changing lanes without using your turn signal."

Hmm. I didn't even know that was against the law. Until that moment I thought using the turn signal was a courtesy.

"I thought that was a courtesy," I said.

"Yeah, well you're wrong," he said as he climbed on his bike.

Eighteen years without a blemish on my record, and I got a ticket for failing to use my turn signal! I gripped my steering wheel hard. And then I remembered the words of my youngest son Paul. The memory triggered an involuntary spasm of my hands, and I gripped my steering wheel harder. I ground my teeth and banged my head on my hands, which held the top of the steering wheel.

"Dad, did you know it's against the law to change lanes without using your turn signal?" Paul had asked. "I thought you'd like to know since you've been switching from one lane to another without using it." He'd uttered those words just six months earlier. I had heard what he said but his words didn't register—until I sat there banging my head.

So I paid a fine for breaking a law that I didn't even know existed. Of course during those spotless eighteen years I deserved many tickets. I had violated traffic laws 11,763 times. I just never got caught. And every time I broke a speeding law, I knew if I got caught I'd have to pay a fine. That's the way life works. Right? Do the crime, pay the fine.

Yet I'm suggesting you break six rules and saying you'll be rewarded for it. I'm insisting that joy comes with grace and freedom, not rules and punishment. I know Jesus would tell you the same thing. The apostle Paul discovered that truth. For years he proudly served as a Pharisee, obsessively obeying Jewish rules and regulations, even hunting down people who violated those rules. Yet one day he met the risen Christ who liberated him from the chains of legalism.

Infused by God's grace, Paul possessed the strength to never again submit to the yoke of man-made rules. His life became a testimony to the joy experienced by the man who consistently breaks these six rules. In case you think I'm exaggerating, consider how he broke the rules outlined in this book:

▶ *The Rule of Passivity: Never Get in a Fight.* Paul publicly confronted Peter when he compelled Gentile believers to follow Jewish traditions (Galatians 2:11-14).

▶ *The Rule of Playing It Safe: Never Risk It All.* Paul risked everything when he embraced the gospel of grace and rejected legalism. In Colossians 2:16-17 (NLT) he said, "Don't let anyone condemn you for what you eat or drink, or for not celebrating certain holy days. . . . For these rules are only shadows of the reality yet to come. And Christ himself is that reality." His stance angered many Jews, and he often paid the price. After preaching in Antioch, "the Jews incited the God-fearing women of high standing and the leading men of the city. They stirred up persecution against Paul and Barnabas, and expelled them from their region" (Acts 13:50).

▶ *The Rule of Perseverance: Never Give Up* and *The Rule of Independence: Never Ask for Help.* Paul didn't cling to his impressive religious credentials and Jewish ancestry but said he considered them worthless compared to the unsurpassed greatness of knowing Christ (see Philippians 3:3-14).

▶ *The Rule of Restraint: Never Lose Your Cool.* Paul expressed his anger when he discovered some of the Corinthian believers were filing lawsuits against one another (1 Corinthians 6:1-8). He obviously got mad at Barnabas and the two even parted company for a while (Acts 15:36-41).

► *The Rule of Impressing Others: Never Look Stupid.* Paul's entire life spoke of a man devoted to pleasing God alone. After encountering Jesus on the road to Damascus, he willingly laid aside his reputation to serve Christ. His letters testify to God's supernatural power at work within him. Yet at the same time, he understood that he and his fellow Christians would look stupid to others. He even told the Corinthians that the message of the cross is "foolishness to those who are perishing" (1 Corinthians 1:18).

The reason I got a ticket is because I broke a legitimate law. Changing lanes without using a turn signal puts other drivers and me at risk. It didn't matter whether I knew the law or not. That regulation was warranted.

The six rules I'm urging you to break, however, are illegitimate. They're phantom rules. Mirages. They're not God-given but man-made. Breaking them may earn you the ire of some Christians. But breaking them will also bring you freedom . . . and with freedom, joy. So go ahead . . . unclip the leash and turn yourself over to the grace of God.

CHECK OUT THESE BOOKS

As you read *6 Rules Every Man Must Break*, you may have identified one or two rules that represent a particular struggle for you. Or perhaps, like me, you wrestle with all of them from time to time. If so, I encourage you to do some further reading. I have recommended a book or two that correspond to the theme of each chapter. Every book below has influenced my own life significantly. I think they'll impact you as well.

Introduction: A Dog Named El Niño
Since I named this chapter after a dog, I thought about suggesting a book on dog training. Instead I'm going to suggest you read one of the two best books I've read in the last year: *The Barbarian Way* by Erwin Raphael McManus and *Blue Like Jazz* by Donald Miller. If you read one of these books and don't like it, I'll refund you the price of the book. (This is only good for the first two people who request a refund . . . and I get to keep the book. Of course, I'm in the witness protection program and nobody knows how to reach me.)

Chapter One: The Rule of Passivity . . . Never Get in a Fight
Paul Coughlin has written an edgy book entitled *No More Christian Nice Guy*, in which he argues that men need to be good instead of nice. He exposes how Christian men have been received into thinking that it's wrong to be masculine and strong. He also demonstrates how Jesus wasn't always the nicest guy in town.

Chapter Two: The Rule of Playing It Safe . . . Never Risk It All
Steve Brown has been hammering home the message of grace for decades. In his book *A Scandalous Freedom*, he insists that many Christians don't trust freedom—for themselves or others. He hits the sweet spot when he notes that men prefer man-made regulations to the adventure of freedom. But he goes further by explaining how men can find true joy through spiritual freedom.

For more insight and encouragement in the area of giving I'd recommend Andy Stanley's *Fields of Gold,* a short, easy read. Andy addressed some of my fears about money—specifically about giving away more money—and helped me discover that giving is an invitation from God.

Chapter Three: The Rule of Perseverance . . . Never Give Up

I realize the *Prayer of Jabez* by Bruce Wilkinson was a best seller and almost everyone on the planet has read it. But there's a reason for that . . . it's an excellent book. If you haven't read it yet, buy a copy and set aside an hour or two to read the entire book. Yes, it's that short. And it will encourage you to break the rule of perseverance . . . to give up trying to make yourself grow spiritually . . . and trust Christ to transform you.

Chapter Four: The Rule of Independence . . . Never Ask for Help

Stu Webber has done a great job with his book *Tender Warrior.* He'll help you realize how to find your identity in Christ and live out your calling as a man of God.

Chapter Five: The Rule of Restraint . . . Never Lose Your Cool

If you'd like to learn more about the concept of anger I wrote about in chapter 5, I urge you to read *The Other Side of Love* by Gary Chapman. This is the best book on anger I've ever read and gave me some seeds for thought that germinated in this chapter.

Chapter Six: The Rule of Impressing Others . . . Never Look Stupid

John Ortberg writes with powerful insight and quick humor. His book *If You Want to Walk on Water, You've Got to Get Out of the Boat* has the longest title allowed on a book cover. But if you're considering a change in your life and fear you might fail, his book is a "must read"!

JOIN THE MOVEMENT

Several years ago I read the story of David's mighty men (found in 1 Samuel 22:1-2 and 2 Samuel 23) and sensed God calling me to get out of my boat and encourage men to become spiritual warriors. I launched a ministry called Million Mighty Men with the belief that if enough men stand together with a common cause and devotion, God's grace would be unleashed in a powerful way. My vision is for a million men to say: "I want to daily engage in the six battles of a mighty man, and I want to lock arms with others who share my desire for spiritual victory."

I hope you'll stand with us. You can do this by going to http://www.6rules.net and entering your name and e-mail address. You'll receive a weekly e-mail from me and become part of a movement of men who have decided to lock arms and fight hypocrisy and legalism. We're committed to winning the battle for our hearts, our families, and others we care for.

I'm also seeking to unite men in an effort to extend the love of God to orphans in India. Together we can make a difference for eternity.

If you want more information about our work with the orphans, or hosting a 6 Rules Every Man Must Break or a Six Battles Every Man Must Win event in your church, community, or ministry, please contact me at: bill@sixbattles.com or P.O. Box 415, Marylhurst, OR 97036. I look forward to hearing from you and hopefully meeting you one day.

ENDNOTES

1. Bill Perkins, *Six Battles Every Man Must Win* (Wheaton, IL.: Tyndale House, 2004), 23.

2. The complete account of Jesus' clash with the Pharisees and the disciples' response can be found in Matthew 15:1-20.

3. Malachi 3:9-10 says, "'You are under a curse—the whole nation of you—because you are robbing me. Bring the whole tithe into the storehouse, that there may be food in my house. 'Test me in this,' says the Lord Almighty, 'and see if I will not throw open the floodgates of heaven and pour out so much blessing that you will not have room enough for it.'"

This passage is often used today to prompt believers to give their tithes to the local church. The idea is that the church today has replaced the Temple as the "storehouse" for tithes. Following this logic, a failure to tithe to the local church would be stealing from God.

It's important to remember that this message was not written for Christians. It was addressed to "the whole nation" (Malachi 3:9).

4. For more information on one of my favorite sources of green coffee beans—and information on how to roast them—check out http://www.sweetmarias.com.

5. Ken Gentry, dean of faculty and professor of systematic theology at Westminster Classical College, has written some thorough and thought-provoking articles on Scripture's stance toward the moderate use of alcohol. These have helped me formulate my own convictions on this topic. His book *God Gave Wine* (Oakdown, 2001) covers this subject in much greater depth than I can in this book. I encourage you to read it if you'd like more biblical insight on the subject.

6. From a letter to the editor of *The Daily Telegraph* (September 23, 1874), written by Charles Spurgeon.

7. Perkins, *Six Battles*, 131.

8. In John 15:2, the verb "cut off" comes from the Greek word *airo*. It should be translated "lifts up." The meaning is consistent with the verse, and nowhere else in the New Testament or other Greek literature does the word mean "cut off." For more on this, see Bruce Wilkinson,

Secrets of the Vine: Breaking Through to Abundance (Sisters, OR: Multnomah Publishers, Inc., 2001), 33.

9. Perkins, *Six Battles*, 135.

10. Merriam-Webster Online Dictionary.

11. Gary Chapman, *The Other Side of Love* (Chicago: Moody Press, 1999), 19.

12. Ibid., 20.

13. Ibid., 21

14. W. E. Vine, *Vine's Expository Dictionary of New Testament Words* (McLean, VA: MacDonald Publishing Company, 1940), 57.

15. Chapman, *The Other Side of Love*, 183.

16. From the *MasterWriter* software program, MasterWriter Inc., copyright © 2002.

17. John Ortberg, *If You Want to Walk on Water, You've Got to Get Out of the Boat* (Grand Rapids, MI: Zondervan, 2001), 17.

SIX BATTLES EVERY MAN MUST WIN

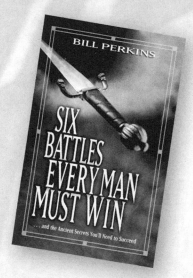

Every day men are confronted with cultural messages that, if accepted, can leave men feeling like failures and adrift from their spiritual focus. Speaker and author Bill Perkins offers hard-earned wisdom on tackling the real challenges men face today. With refreshing honesty, Bill chronicles his own struggles with disappointment, failure, and depression and tells how the little-known biblical story of David's "mighty men" transformed his life. Bill's battle cry will help to strengthen and inspire men to stand up against the unseen—but deadly—enemies without fear.

LEADERSHIP ABOVE THE LINE

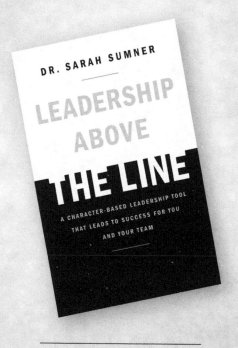

If you're working "above the line," you're in your unique success zone—leading with excellence and character in the way that best fits your strengths. *Leadership above the Line* uses Jesus as the model of the ideal balanced leader. Dr. Sarah Sumner offers practical tools to help you incorporate above-the-line strengths into your everyday life. Available everywhere books are sold.